SO YOU WANT TO BUILD A HUMAN?

The Ultimate HUMAN BODY MANUAL

Tom Jackson ● Illustrated by Jan Bielecki

WELBECK

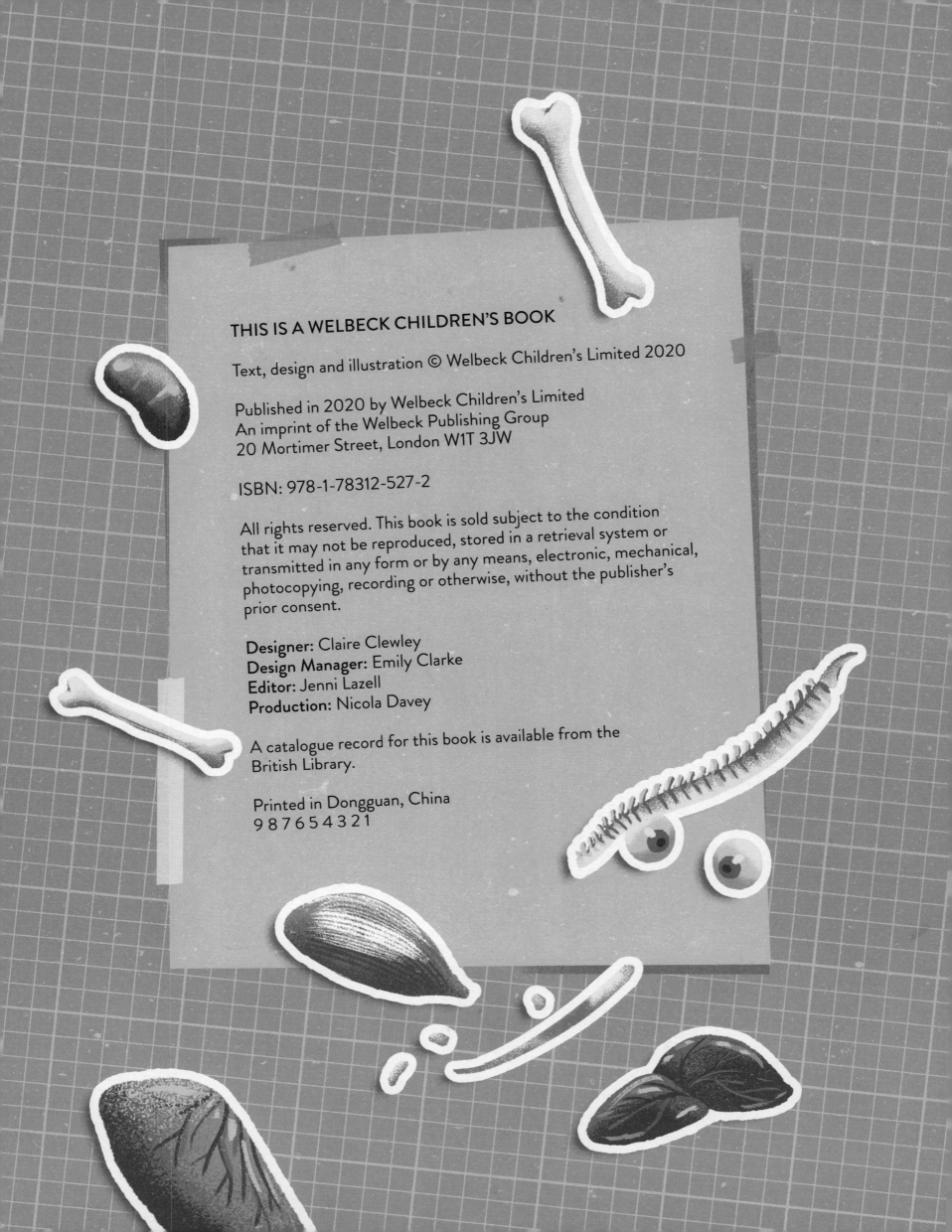

THIS IS A WELBECK CHILDREN'S BOOK

Text, design and illustration © Welbeck Children's Limited 2020

Published in 2020 by Welbeck Children's Limited
An imprint of the Welbeck Publishing Group
20 Mortimer Street, London W1T 3JW

ISBN: 978-1-78312-527-2

Designer: Claire Clewley
Design Manager: Emily Clarke
Editor: Jenni Lazell
Production: Nicola Davey

A catalogue record for this book is available from the British Library.

Printed in Dongguan, China
9 8 7 6 5 4 3 2 1

CONTENTS

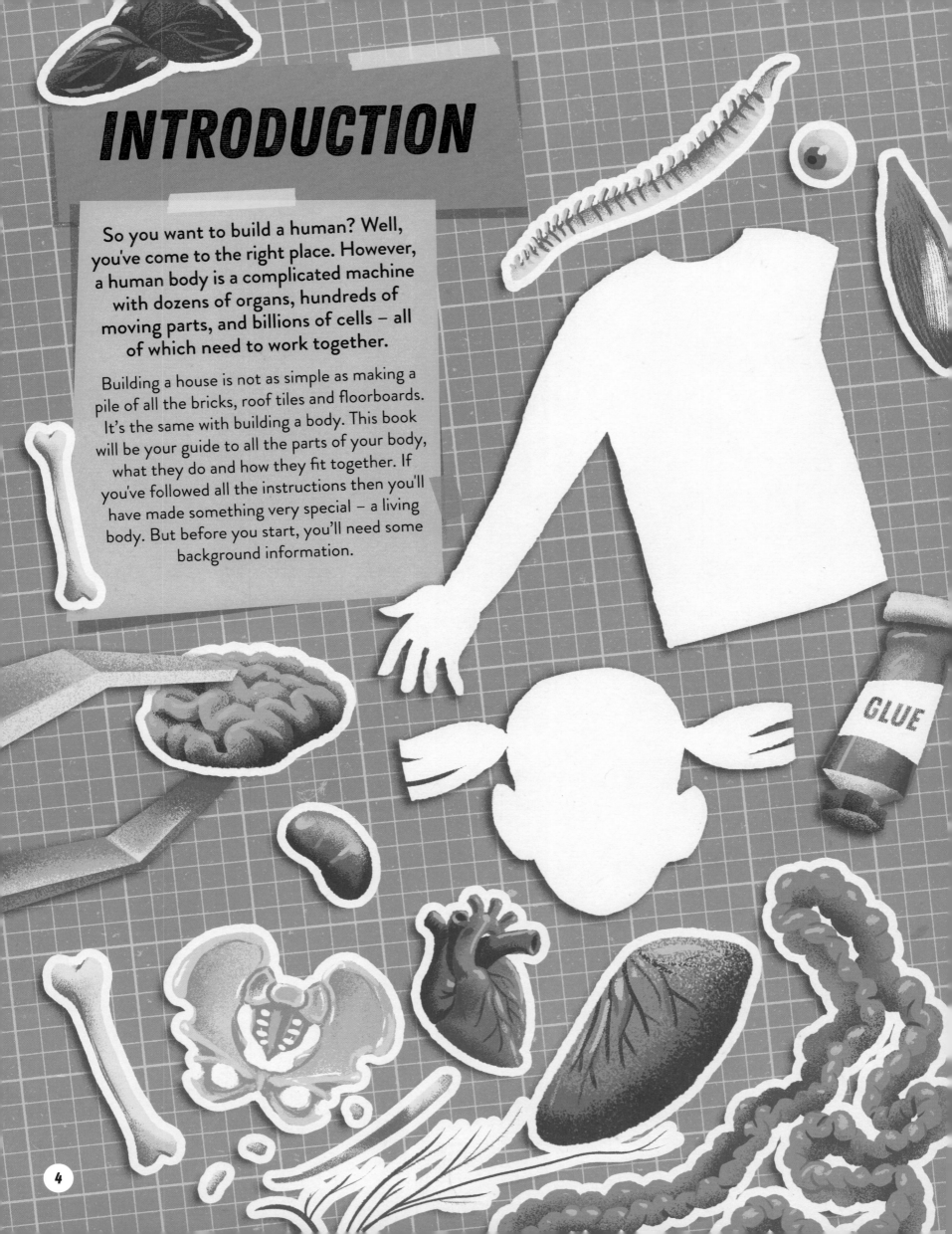

INTRODUCTION

So you want to build a human? Well, you've come to the right place. However, a human body is a complicated machine with dozens of organs, hundreds of moving parts, and billions of cells – all of which need to work together.

Building a house is not as simple as making a pile of all the bricks, roof tiles and floorboards. It's the same with building a body. This book will be your guide to all the parts of your body, what they do and how they fit together. If you've followed all the instructions then you'll have made something very special – a living body. But before you start, you'll need some background information.

GLUE

Getting organised

A healthy human body has to be highly organised, and work at different sizes within the body.

Cells: At the smallest scale are the cells. These are building blocks that are used to make everything in the body. An adult man's body contains about 30 trillion cells – and a quarter of those are red blood cells.

Tissues: Cells are specialised to do a certain job, and they work in teams called tissues. Bones, muscles or nerves are tissues made up from sets of very different cells.

Organs: Tissues also get organised to do more complicated tasks and can form a body part called an organ. The brain and the heart are the most important organs – although there are many others that we would struggle to do without.

Body system: This is the top level of organisation, where the organs link together to carry out the body's biggest jobs, like digestion, movement, excretion and reproduction – in other words the stuff that makes the body alive.

Raw ingredients

A living body is made from the same materials as non-living stuff, like cars and rocks, only it is all arranged in a different way. The raw ingredients are simply substances called elements. More than 98 per cent of the body is made up of just six elements – as shown in this pie chart.

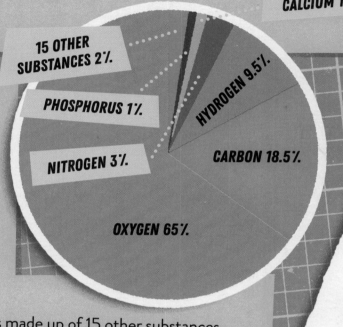

CALCIUM 1%.
15 OTHER SUBSTANCES 2%.
PHOSPHORUS 1%.
HYDROGEN 9.5%.
NITROGEN 3%.
CARBON 18.5%.
OXYGEN 65%.

The other 2 per cent is made up of 15 other substances such as iron, sodium, and sulphur. These are used in only very tiny amounts – a few thousandths of a gram – but without them the body would not work properly.

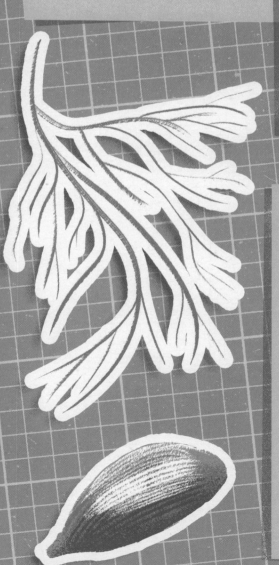

What is life?

How can you tell if something is alive? Some things might seem obvious, like a puppy, but what about a tree, a rock or a car? A car can move and burn fuel, but it can't grow or produce baby cars, so it is not alive (phew!). There are some simple tests to help you work out if something is alive:

- **Movement:** At least part of it can move by itself.
- **Excretion:** Waste materials are removed.
- **Energy:** Nutrients from food are burned to release energy.
- **Reproduction:** It can produce offspring.
- **Sensory awareness:** Being able to detect changes in the surroundings and respond to them.
- **Nutrition:** It can collect a supply of food from outside itself.
- **Growth:** It can get bigger (at least to start with) and is able to carry out repairs.

SKELETON
The Support System

It's always good to start with the really hard stuff. Most of your body parts are squidgy, so you'll need a tough frame to keep the body in shape. That is the job of the skeleton; without it you wouldn't be able to stand or move around.

The human skeleton is made of 206 bones, mostly connected together by stretchy bands called ligaments. A bone might look like a rocky stick, but it is very much alive. It gets its hardness from a chalky chemical called calcium phosphate. The outside looks solid but inside the bone is full of tiny holes. This spongy set-up keeps the bone's strength but reduces its weight.

Spine

The spine, or backbone, is made up of 33 interlocking units, each one known as a vertebra. Together they make a flexible snake of bone that lets the body twist and bend. The spine also protects the spinal cord, a thick cable of nerves that connects the brain to the body.

The smallest bone in the body, the stirrup, is in the ear. It is just 3 millimetres long.

↓
Stirrup
(actual size)

KEEP THE LOWER JAWBONE, OR MANDIBLE, SEPARATE FROM THE SKULL. IT NEEDS TO MOVE EASILY FOR CHEWING.

Skull

This bony brainbox is made of 22 curved bones, all fused together to create a protective case around the brain. The skull has several holes in it to let nerves and blood vessels in and out, plus two sockets for the eyes.

Ribs

This set of 24 bones curves around from the spine to form a protective cage around the body's most vital parts: the heart, lungs, stomach and other major organs.

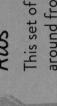

Pelvis

Six chunky bones form a girdle, or ring shape, around the base of the body. This sturdy structure connects to the spine and the legs. The coccyx, or tailbone, at the base of the spine is all that is left of our monkey tail.

The strongest bone in the body is the thigh bone, or femur. It can hold 30 times the weight of the body.

A newborn baby has 305 bones. The bones are soft and bendy, but as the baby grows, the bones harden and fuse together to make 206 adult bones.

The foot

This is the only part of the body that is built for taking your whole weight. It has a similar set of bones as the hand but they are not as moveable. Instead they are locked together into a springy platform that is perfect for walking and running.

The hand

Each hand has 27 bones in it, which explains why it is so flexible in all directions. The human thumb can reach across the palm and touch the pinky finger, which means our hands can grip very tightly but also be very gentle at small delicate tasks.

Arms and legs

The arms and legs are all made from the same number of bones, all arranged in the same pattern, but don't get them muddled up – the leg bones are longer and thicker.

The inner core of big bones is called bone marrow. This fatty section is where red blood cells are made.

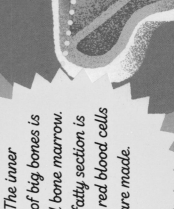

7

BRAIN
The Control Centre

The human body is complicated, that much is easy to see. So how come it works so well? The main reason is right there between your ears – the brain. The brain is a busy piece of equipment that controls all body processes, and it is where your mind is located – the bit of the body that thinks and has ideas about stuff.

Although it's made mostly from wobbly fat, inside the brain there are 83 billion brain cells, or neurons, each connected to many thousands of neighbouring cells. Scientists think that there are around 100 trillion connections in the brain, and the more connections a brain has, the smarter it is. This makes the human brain the most complicated thing in the Universe!

Temporal lobe

Located on the left and right side, this part handles information from the senses and is one of the main regions for handling memories.

Frontal lobe

The forward part of the brain is there to do the thinking, make decisions and plan what the body should do next. It contains the motor cortex, which is the command centre for body movements.

The part of the brain that handles information is called grey matter. The brain also has white matter, which forms the connections between sections of the brain.

Parietal lobe

The top part is concerned with keeping track of where the body is, what's around it and what position it is in. The parietal lobe contains the sensory cortex, which receives signals from all the senses. This important information is then sent to the frontal lobe for action.

THE BRAIN IS IN TWO HALVES, OR HEMISPHERES, WHICH SHARE JOBS OUT BETWEEN THEM. MAKE SURE THEY CAN SWAP INFORMATION BY CONNECTING THEM IN THE MIDDLE.

SYSTEMS CHECK

WEIGHT: *1.5 kg*

FUNCTION: *The control centre for all body processes*

CONTROL: *Manages everything from breathing and sleeping to thinking and talking*

IMPORTANCE: *Without your brain you would not be you*

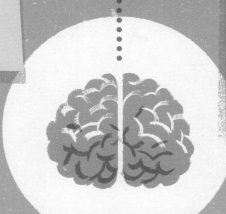

Occipital lobe

Located at the back of the brain, this part is the vision mixer. It makes pictures of the world using signals coming from the eyes, but also adds in information from memories to create a simple and clear view of the world.

The brain makes up about 2 per cent of the body's weight but uses 20 per cent of energy.

Cerebellum

With a name that means 'little brain', the cerebellum is the motion control system. It contains pre-recorded movements, such as walking, running, playing sports or riding a bike, which are sent out to the body to be put into action when commanded by the frontal lobes.

Brain stem

The lower part of the brain, also called the brain stem, is in charge of the most basic body processes, such as breathing, heartbeat and swallowing food. This is the bit that keeps the body alive, and sometimes keeps on working even when the rest of the brain has stopped.

MUSCLES
Get Moving

It's time to get a move on, and for that you will need some muscles. There are three types of muscle: skeletal, smooth and cardiac.

Muscles are made of two kinds of proteins, one thick and one thin, which overlap each other to make a fleshy fibre. When given an electric signal, the thin proteins haul themselves along the thick ones, and that makes the fibre contract and get shorter. Every movement in the body is made by a muscle's pulling power. But muscles cannot *push* so they have to work in pairs. Shall we start putting it all together?

There are 650 skeletal muscles attached to bones.

Skeletal muscle

The muscles used to move the body are packed full of protein bundles. Up close they look striped. Skeletal muscles are under voluntary control, which means you can decide when to move them, or not.

Smooth muscle

These muscles are all over the body, especially in the stomach and intestines, but also in the airways and blood vessels. The muscles form into rings or flat sheets and often contract in sync to make rippling effects, which helps push food or blood along. Smooth muscles always run on automatic control and get to work without us having to think about it.

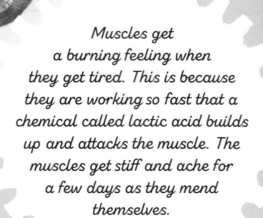

Muscles get a burning feeling when they get tired. This is because they are working so fast that a chemical called lactic acid builds up and attacks the muscle. The muscles get stiff and ache for a few days as they mend themselves.

Joints

Every muscle pair is set up to move a flexible section of the skeleton called a joint. There are six types, all of which allow us to move parts of the body in different ways. For example: hinge joints in our elbows let us move them up and down only, while ball and socket joints in our shoulders allow us to make large movements in all directions.

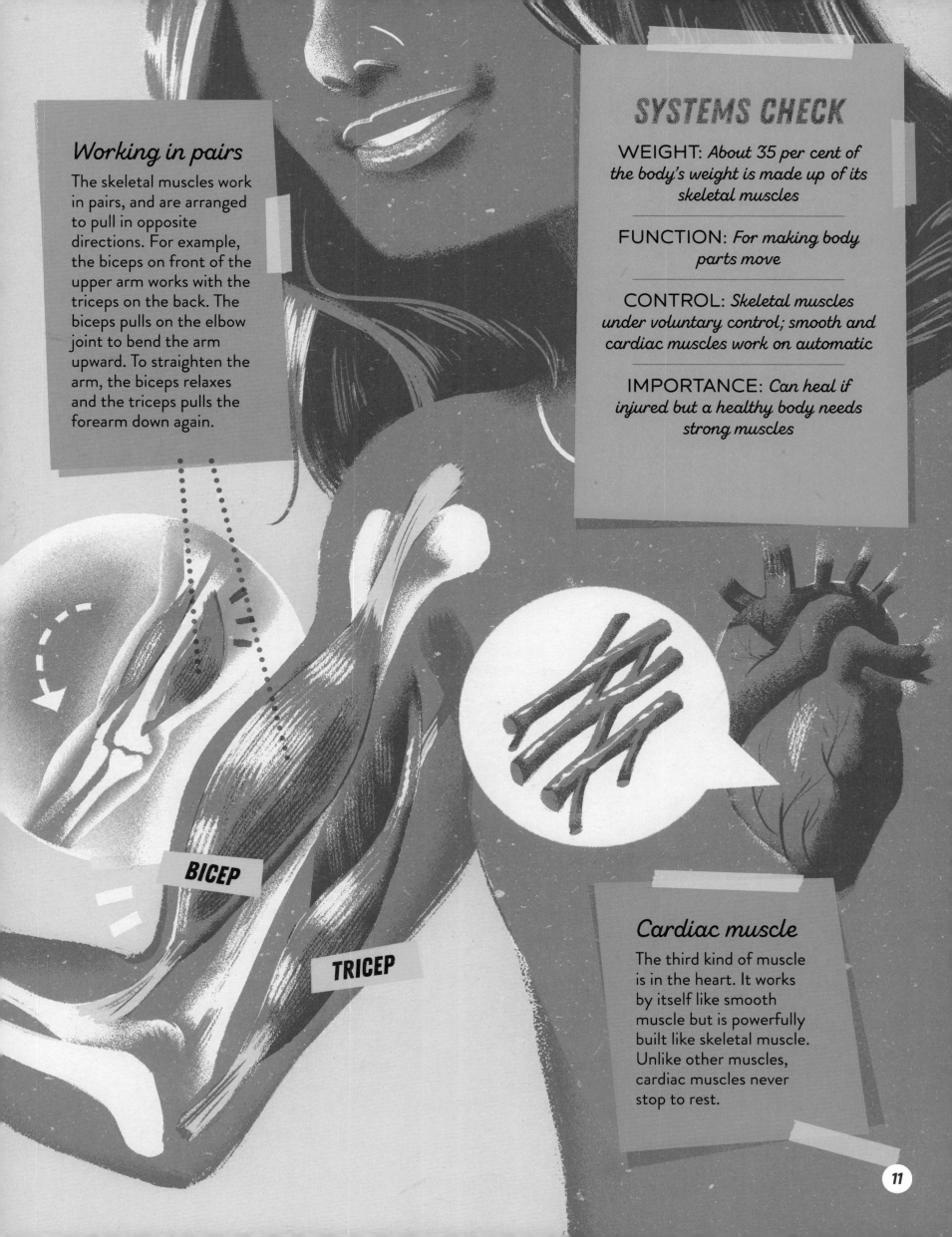

Working in pairs

The skeletal muscles work in pairs, and are arranged to pull in opposite directions. For example, the biceps on front of the upper arm works with the triceps on the back. The biceps pulls on the elbow joint to bend the arm upward. To straighten the arm, the biceps relaxes and the triceps pulls the forearm down again.

SYSTEMS CHECK

WEIGHT: *About 35 per cent of the body's weight is made up of its skeletal muscles*

FUNCTION: *For making body parts move*

CONTROL: *Skeletal muscles under voluntary control; smooth and cardiac muscles work on automatic*

IMPORTANCE: *Can heal if injured but a healthy body needs strong muscles*

BICEP

TRICEP

Cardiac muscle

The third kind of muscle is in the heart. It works by itself like smooth muscle but is powerfully built like skeletal muscle. Unlike other muscles, cardiac muscles never stop to rest.

HEART AND BLOOD SUPPLY
The Transporter

Shhh! What can you hear? Nothing, that's what. Let's fix that by adding a beating heart to thump out a rhythm for the body. The heart will need a circulatory system of blood vessels filled with about 5 litres of blood for an adult body.

The pumping of the heart pushes the blood to every corner of the body, and the whole lot goes all the way around in less than a minute. The blood works like a continuous conveyor belt that delivers what body parts need and takes away the leftovers. End-to-end, a body's blood vessels would stretch 100,000 kilometres – about a quarter of the way to the Moon!

When seen through thin skin, veins can look blue or green, but the blood inside is always red.

Four chambers

The heart is divided into two halves, left and right. Each side has an upper chamber, called the atrium, and a lower, larger one called the ventricle. The right-hand chambers collect blood from the body and send it to the lungs, while the left side receives fresh blood from the lungs and pumps it out into the body.

RIGHT ATRIUM

Beat: The system

When the heart beats, each pair of atria and ventricles work as a team. Blood arrives into the atria. These fill up and then valves to the ventricles open, and the atria muscles contract, squeezing blood into the ventricles. The valves close and the ventricles contract, pumping the blood out of the heart again. This double contraction creates the lub-dub sound of the heart beat.

CHECK THE SYSTEM IS WORKING BY FEELING FOR A PULSE, WHICH IS THE MUSCULAR PUMPING OF AN ARTERY. YOU CAN FEEL THIS WHERE AN ARTERY IS CLOSE TO THE SKIN, SUCH AS IN THE WRIST OR NECK.

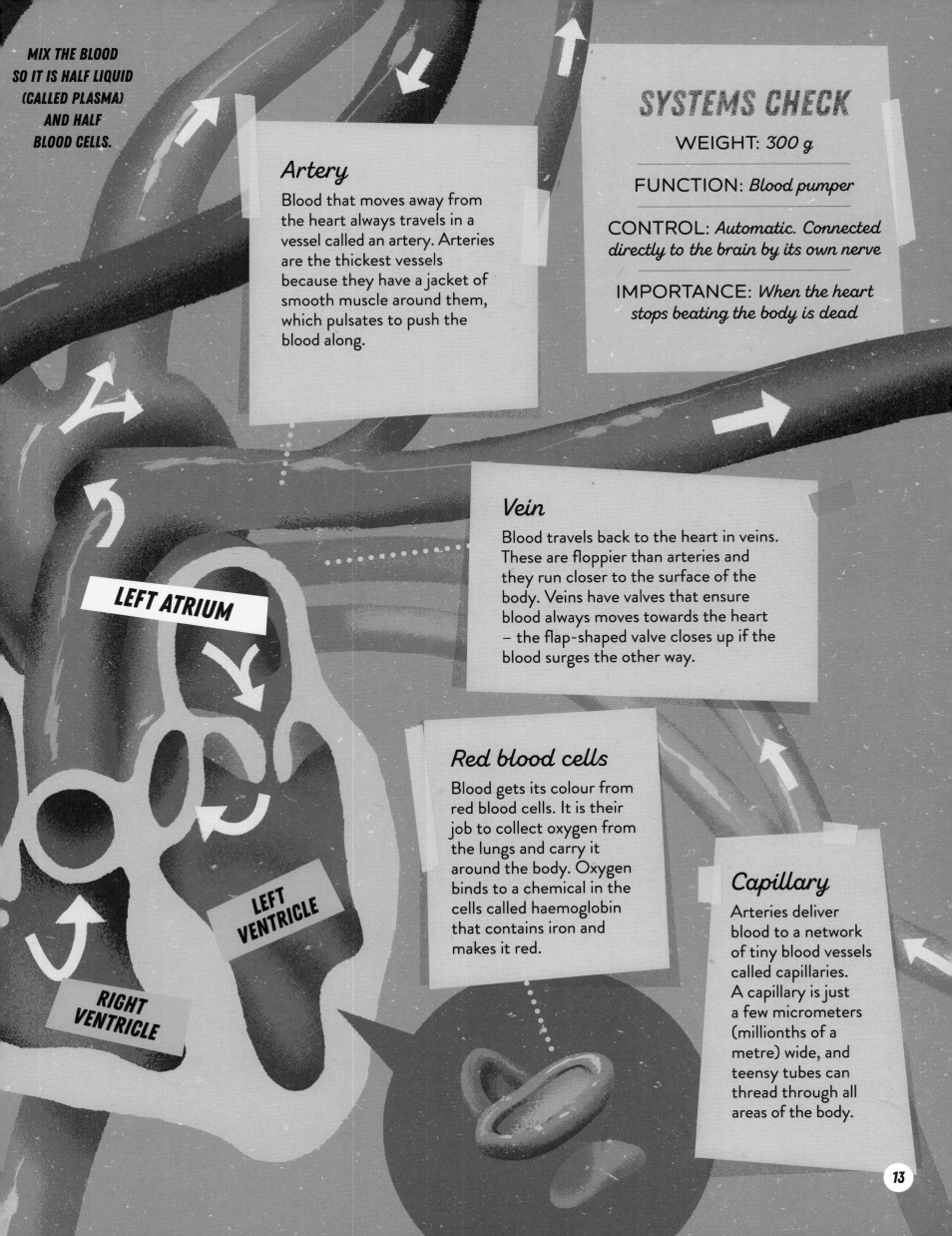

MIX THE BLOOD SO IT IS HALF LIQUID (CALLED PLASMA) AND HALF BLOOD CELLS.

Artery

Blood that moves away from the heart always travels in a vessel called an artery. Arteries are the thickest vessels because they have a jacket of smooth muscle around them, which pulsates to push the blood along.

SYSTEMS CHECK

WEIGHT: *300 g*

FUNCTION: *Blood pumper*

CONTROL: *Automatic. Connected directly to the brain by its own nerve*

IMPORTANCE: *When the heart stops beating the body is dead*

Vein

Blood travels back to the heart in veins. These are floppier than arteries and they run closer to the surface of the body. Veins have valves that ensure blood always moves towards the heart – the flap-shaped valve closes up if the blood surges the other way.

LEFT ATRIUM

LEFT VENTRICLE

RIGHT VENTRICLE

Red blood cells

Blood gets its colour from red blood cells. It is their job to collect oxygen from the lungs and carry it around the body. Oxygen binds to a chemical in the cells called haemoglobin that contains iron and makes it red.

Capillary

Arteries deliver blood to a network of tiny blood vessels called capillaries. A capillary is just a few micrometers (millionths of a metre) wide, and teensy tubes can thread through all areas of the body.

13

LUNGS
Air Supply

It's been hard work so far. Perhaps it's time to have a rest and catch our breath. But for that you'll need a pair of lungs.

The lungs are located in the chest, either side of the heart, and it's their job to collect oxygen from the air. This gas is used by the body to burn sugars and other foods to release the energy the body needs to stay alive. That is why we cannot hold our breath for very long – we need a constant supply of oxygen. This whole process is called respiration, and the lungs are the main part of the respiratory system. We better fit a pair right now.

Windpipe

Air moves in and out of the lungs via a stiff tube called the windpipe (the proper name is trachea). The windpipe connects with the throat and then on to the air outside through the mouth and nostrils. It has a little flap called the epiglottis, which slams shut to stop food and drink going down into the lungs by mistake.

Coughs and sneezes

It is important to keep the airways and lungs free of blockages. When the windpipe has something in it – normally just some snot – the lungs take in a big breath, but the epiglottis stays shut during the out breath. Then at the last minute it opens and a blast of air is released, making a coughing noise that clears the blockage. In a sneeze, the same kind of thing happens, although this time the tongue directs all the air out the nose – clearing the nostrils in a spray of snot!

A sneeze forces air out of the nose at a speed of about 160 km per hour – that's faster than a cheetah can run!

When resting we take about 15 breaths every minute, which adds up to breathing in 13,500 litres of air every day.

Tube network

The windpipe divides into two tubes called bronchi that connect to the left and right lung. The bronchi divide into narrower and narrower tubes called bronchioles, which branch out inside the lung. Each bronchiole ends with a tiny air sac called an alveolus. The alveolus is surrounded by capillaries where the air meets the blood supply and gases are exchanged. Oxygen goes from the air to the blood, and carbon dioxide, which is the waste gas produced by the body, comes out of the blood into the air.

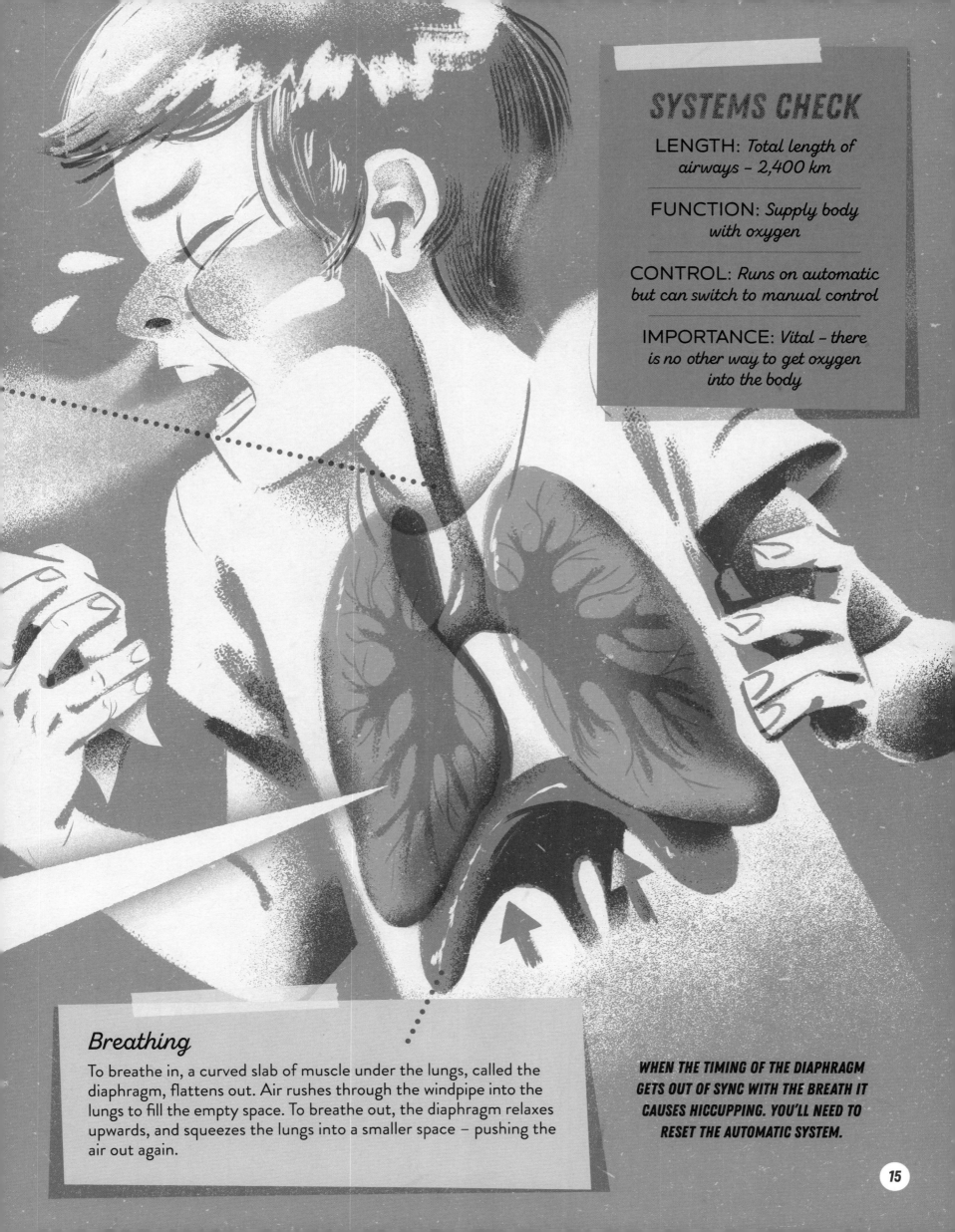

Breathing

To breathe in, a curved slab of muscle under the lungs, called the diaphragm, flattens out. Air rushes through the windpipe into the lungs to fill the empty space. To breathe out, the diaphragm relaxes upwards, and squeezes the lungs into a smaller space – pushing the air out again.

WHEN THE TIMING OF THE DIAPHRAGM GETS OUT OF SYNC WITH THE BREATH IT CAUSES HICCUPPING. YOU'LL NEED TO RESET THE AUTOMATIC SYSTEM.

DIGESTIVE SYSTEM
The Food Processor

Feeling hungry? In that case you're going to need a digestive system. This is a long tube that twists and turns inside the body, starting at the mouth and ending at the, ahem, bottom.

The digestive system's many parts break up the food and take out any useful parts for fuelling the rest of the body. That leaves a lump of useless waste, and you'll also already know what happens to that. Let's put the digestive system together.

It takes between 12 and 48 hours for a meal to travel right through the digestive system.

Oesophagus

Also called the gullet, this pipe takes the food to the stomach. Like the rest of the digestive system, it has muscular walls that squeeze in and out to push the food along.

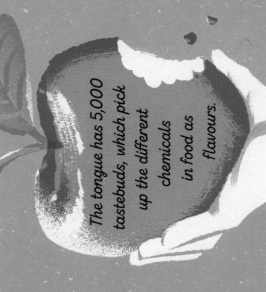

The tongue has 5,000 tastebuds, which pick up the different chemicals in food as flavours.

Mouth

The teeth slice and grind the food, which is also mixed with spit to create a soft mush that is easy to swallow.

Stomach

The stomach is a bag of muscle where the food mush is mixed with acids and other chemicals and then given a good shake. After about four hours, the solid food has been broken down into a thick liquid.

The stomach can swell up to ten times its size after a big meal.

Rectum

The rectum is used for getting rid of food waste. It works like an airlock on a space station. The inner opening lets in poo from the intestine. It then closes, and the outer one opens up for the poo to plop out. Are you still feeling hungry now?

KEEP THIS VALVE TIGHTLY SHUT OR ACID FROM THE STOMACH WILL LEAK OUT CAUSING INDIGESTION.

The acid in the stomach is powerful enough to dissolve steel (but very slowly).

Small Intestine

The stomach liquid then goes to the small intestine, where its useful parts are collected by the blood. We call it 'small' because this intestine is only 3 centimetres wide, but it is actually about 6 metres long. If its frilly inner surface was spread flat it would cover a tennis court!

REMEMBER – THE SMALL INTESTINE GOES BEFORE THE LARGE ONE.

Large Intestine

The leftovers, a thin watery waste, splosh into the large intestine, where they are pumped up and around in a loop. The water is gradually taken back into the body leaving behind a soft lump of poo.

LIVER
The Chemical Factory

Next we will add the hardest-working organ in the body – the liver.

Often overlooked, the liver just beats the brain to being the largest and heaviest organ inside the body. It looks like a red-brown lump that sits under the lungs, but don't be fooled by its quiet appearance. The liver is doing many different things all at once. Its main role is to form the link between the digestive system and the blood supply. It is a tough piece of equipment, making safe the poisons that get into the body – and mending itself when it gets damaged.

The liver recycles old red blood cells and adds them to the bile. This makes the bile greenish yellow when mixed with other chemicals. It then passes through the rest of the digestive system and gives poo its brown colour.

Four lobes

The liver fits snugly under the diaphragm and shares the space above the intestines with the stomach. As a result the liver has a triangular shape to leave some room for the stomach on the left. It is divided into four sections called lobes, which are all different sizes and shaped to fill whatever space is available. The right lobe is the largest and is separated from the left one by two smaller lumps. Each lobe is filled with tiny blood vessels, which surround a solid mass of smaller structures called lobules. That is where all the hard work is done.

The liver adds fibrin to the blood. This is the chemical that turns blood into solid scabs that block up a cut in the skin.

Portal vein

This is a very special blood vessel that connects the intestines to the liver, and about three quarters of the liver's blood comes through it. It is not really a vein at all, because it does not take blood to the heart. Instead the portal vein transports all the useful chemicals extracted from our food. The liver then turns it into materials for the body to use, which are then mixed into the blood and sent into the body.

THE LIVER HAS A HUGE BLOOD SUPPLY. MAKE SURE THE BLOOD COMING IN ARRIVES FROM THE AORTA, THE LARGEST ARTERY IN THE BODY, AND THEN LEAVES BY THE VENA CAVA, THE LARGEST VEIN.

Bile works by breaking up fat into tiny blobs, in much the same way that soap breaks up dirt. In fact, the bile collected from dead animals was once used as an early kind of fabric cleaner!

Gallbladder

Near the underside of the liver is a small sac called the gallbladder. This fills with a liquid called bile, which trickles out of the liver. Bile is mixture of salts and oils, and its job is to stop fats forming into lumps in the digestive system.

CONNECT THE GALLBLADDER TO THE SMALL INTESTINE WITH THE BILE DUCT.

Energy store

One of the liver's most important jobs is to process sugar. The digestive system releases simple sugars from food, and the body uses it as the main source of energy. These tiny molecules are ideal for mixing into the blood and spreading around the body quickly, but they are not easy to store when they are not immediately needed. The liver solves this problem by clustering thousands of sugar molecules into big blobs called glycogen.

KIDNEY AND BLADDER
The Cleaners

The body seems to be working well. But something crucial is missing. The body's metabolism produces chemicals that it cannot find another use for. The by-products of life are often nasty poisons that will make us ill unless the body can get rid of them. You need a way to handle waste.

The body's waste is managed by the excretory system, and its main organs are the kidneys. The kidney is a blood filter and it sifts out unwanted materials making a liquid mixture called urine (or pee). This is stored for a short while in the bladder, until there is a convenient moment to release it from the body. There is no time to waste when it comes to waste.

The main ingredient of urine is a chemical called urea. It is quite poisonous so the body dilutes it in water to make it less harmful. Urea is made in the liver from the unwanted parts of proteins that arrive from the digestive system.

URETERS

Nephron

Each kidney contains thousands of tube systems called nephrons. These are the blood filters that make urine. A tiny squirt of the liquid part of the blood – the plasma – leaks out and runs into each nephron. As the plasma trickles through the twisting tubes, any useful chemicals, such as salt and some of the water, are taken out and put back into the blood. That leaves a watery mixture of unwanted chemicals – urine – that drips into ducts that lead to the ureter and then down to the bladder.

Kidneys

There are two kidneys, located on either side of the body. Both sit behind the intestines and poke out from the bottom of the rib cage. The famously bean-shaped organs are small enough to fit into the palm of your hand. Despite their small size, the kidneys are supplied by thick veins and arteries, which connect directly to the aorta and vena cava – the two thickest blood vessels of all.

Ureter

A third tube coming out of the kidney is the ureter. The ureters carry the urine produced by the kidneys down to the bladder. Each one can be up to 30 centimetres long and they run down behind the intestines and then connect to the top of the bladder, which sits in the middle of the pelvis.

It's better to pee often, but you can hold it in for a long time if you need to. The bladder helps to ease your urges by sending some of the water back into the blood. When you do eventually pee, the urine will appear darker as there are more chemicals mixed into the water.

Bladder

The bladder is a simple organ: it is a bag of muscles with two entry points at the top – the ureters –and one exit point at the bottom, which is called the urethra. The urethra can open up and close tightly again – we learn how to control it as toddlers. The bladder has a capacity of about half a litre. When it gets about half full, the weight of the urine pushing on the urethra makes us begin to feel like we need to pee.

Pee chart

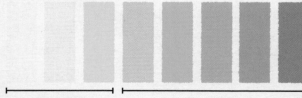

Healthy   Drink more

SKIN
All Surface

On average blonde people have the most hair on their heads and redheads the least.

You now have all the vital organs – the ones that are essential for life. Such important body parts need a bit of protection... A covering of skin should do it.

It is easy to forget about how important the skin is but it is amazing stuff. Imagine a material that is very tough but still really soft and flexible. It is also entirely waterproof and can fix itself if it gets damaged. Only skin can do that – and it has a lot more going besides. Humans are hairy animals – although we are less furry than most other mammals – and the body uses hairs for several different jobs. Let's wrap things up.

Sweat glands

Among all the hairs, the skin has tiny holes called sweat pores. When the body is too hot, salty water pumps out of the pores, making the body sweat. As the sweat evaporates it takes away some of the body's heat, helping it cool down.

Skin layers

As well as providing a barrier that stops germs and dirt getting into the body, the skin also stops useful stuff, like water or blood, from leaking out of the body. It does all this using a three-layered structure.

Epidermis: The outermost layer is mostly made of dead cells. The cells are filled with a waxy substance called keratin, which creates the skin's waterproof layer. The dead cells are always being brushed away and are replaced by new ones, which grow out from underneath. These cells do not get oxygen from the blood, but instead take it from the air – the skin 'breathes'.

Dermis: The next layer is about 5 times thicker than the epidermis. It is made from a mixture of fats and fibres, which make the skin soft but flexible. Most of the touch sensors that allow the skin to feel things are located in the dermis.

Hypodermis: The lowest layer is the connection between the skin above to the bones, muscles and organs below. The body will store fat here if it eats more food than it needs.

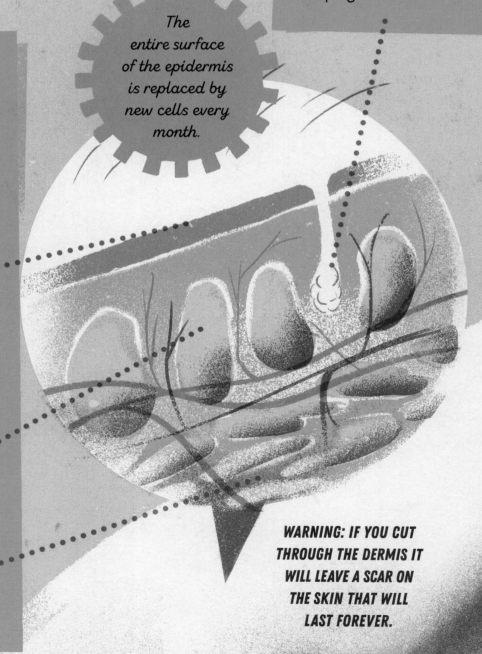

The entire surface of the epidermis is replaced by new cells every month.

WARNING: IF YOU CUT THROUGH THE DERMIS IT WILL LEAVE A SCAR ON THE SKIN THAT WILL LAST FOREVER.

Nails

The finger and toenails are made from keratin. Our nails are our body's equivalent of the claws and hooves in other animals. They help out by making the fingers tougher when ripping into food.

Fingernails grow faster than toenails at around 3 millimetres a month.

FEELING COLD? MAKE SURE TO EQUIP EACH SKIN HAIR WITH A TINY MUSCLE THAT PULLS THEM UPRIGHT. THIS CREATES A HAIRY LAYER ABOVE THE SKIN THAT TRAPS WARM AIR AGAINST THE BODY. THE UPRIGHT HAIRS APPEAR ON THE SKIN AS GOOSEBUMPS.

Hair types

A hair is not made from cells like the rest of the body. Instead it is a shaft of keratin, the same flexible and waterproof chemical that is in skin. Every hair grows from a root, or follicle, embedded in the dermis, but its job depends on where it is in the body.

There are 50 times more hairs growing on the body than on the head, only most are very short and very fine. The longest body hairs are on the scalp. Head hairs grow at about 1 centimetre a month. No one is really sure what this hair is for.

CURLY HAIR: FLAT, OVAL FOLLICE

STRAIGHT HAIR: ROUND FOLLICE

WAVY HAIR: EGG-SHAPED FOLLICE

EYES
The Viewing Station

IN BRIGHT CONDITIONS, USE THE IRIS TO MAKE THE PUPIL SMALLER AND RESTRICT THE LIGHT GETTING IN. WHEN IT'S DARK, OPEN THE IRIS WIDE SO YOU CAN COLLECT AS MUCH LIGHT AS POSSIBLE.

The body is looking pretty good now, can you see? Whoops, we still need to add the eyes!

The human body has just two eyes, both pointing forwards. This is called binocular vision. While some animals have eyes that look sideways so they can see almost all the way around, both human eyes look at the same place at the same time. Tiny differences in the pictures from each eye give the brain important details about the precise shapes of objects and exactly how far away they are. Let's take a closer look.

Lens

Light entering the eye has to be focused. This job is done by the lens: a see-through flexible disc. Tiny muscles pull on the lens, stretching it slightly until its curved shape is just right for making the light form as a single clear image on the back of the eye.

Light in

The eye works just like a camera. It has only one opening at the front, called the pupil, where light enters. When you look into a pupil, it looks very dark. That is because no light is reflected back out.

The internal space of the eye is a clear jelly called the vitreous humour.

Retina

The back of the eye is covered in a layer of light-sensitive cells called the retina. These cells have chemicals in them that react to light and that results in a nerve signal heading for the brain. Each cell on the retina is like one dot in the overall picture. Together these dots build up into a detailed moving image of the surroundings.

RETINA

PUPIL

LENS

CORNEA

IRIS

OPTIC NERVE

The coloured pattern of the iris is as unique to a person as their fingerprints.

PUT IN ENOUGH FUNCTIONING CONE CELLS TO SEE THE NUMBER IN THE COLOURED DOTS.

Rods and Cones

All the cells in the retina connect to the optic nerve, which runs right into the middle of the brain.

Cone cells: There are three types of cone cell. The first is sensitive to red light; another picks up green light, while the third one detects blue light. The brain constructs a colour image using information sent by each type of cone. People (mostly men) who don't have enough cone cells – or they just don't work well – can't tell the difference between certain colours and are known as colour blind.

Rod cell: These cells are ultra sensitive to light, and during the day they shut down. However, at night, when it is too dark for the cone cells to work, the rods can still create an image – but only in black and white.

EARS
The Sound System

What do you say we should build next? I said, "WHAT DO YOU SAY...!" Oh I get it, you can't hear. Here, ears are what you need. The ear is best known as a sound detector, but what are sounds?

Sounds are waves that are squeezing and stretching the air all around us, and they are set in motion when something makes the air wobble. That could be a handclap, a slammed door, or a mouth pushing air through a whistle. Weirdly, the waves are completely silent until they enter the ears, which then turn the wobbling air into nerve signals for our brains to experience as sound.

Outer ear

This fleshy flap is the only part of ear that you can see. It is also called the pinna and is a kind of spiralling funnel that collects sound waves. The waves are channelled down a tube called the ear canal, which leads to the middle ear.

USE LUMPS OF SQUIDGY EARWAX TO SWEEP UP ANY DUST AND GERMS IN THE EAR CANAL. THE WAX WILL CLEAN ITSELF OUT OF THE EAR CANAL. NEVER STICK ANYTHING SMALLER THAN YOUR ELBOW INTO THE EAR!

Some people who struggle to hear wear a hearing aid. This magnifies sound vibrations entering the ear.

Drum skin

The ear canal passes through a little hole in the skull and ends with a wall of skin called the eardrum. The sound wave hits the eardrum, making it wobble with the same rhythm as the wave.

Shell like

The inner ear is a hollow bone shaped into looping tubes and a twisting spiral. It is called the labyrinth and is filled with a jelly liquid. The lower part, the cochlea, looks like the coil of a snail shell. The tap tap tap on the stirrup bone sends ripples into the cochlea. The ripples waft hairlike nerve cells, which convert this motion into a signal that goes to the brain and... you hear a sound!

FITTING ONE EAR ON EITHER SIDE OF THE HEAD WILL BE VERY USEFUL IN TELLING WHERE A SOUND IS COMING FROM. THE NEAREST EAR WILL ALWAYS HEAR THE SOUND FIRST. YOU PROBABLY CAN'T NOTICE THE DIFFERENCE IN TIMINGS, BUT YOUR BRAIN WILL DETECT IT.

SYSTEMS CHECK

LENGTH: *2 cm long*
(ear canal)

FUNCTION: *Hearing*

CONTROL: *Automatic sense organ*

IMPORTANCE: *Very useful, but not essential*

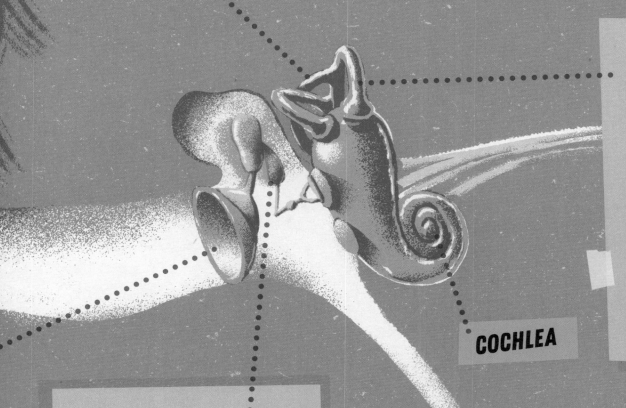

COCHLEA

Staying balanced

The top half of the labyrinth keeps you balanced using tubes called the semicircular canals. Every body movement makes the fluid surge one way or another along these tubes, and that helps the brain organise what muscles are needed to stop you falling over. If you spin around very fast, tiny whirlpools appear in the canals, and you'll feel all confused and dizzy.

Hammer time

The back of the eardrum is connected to a tiny bone called the hammer, which moves with every wobble. The hammer taps against a neighbouring bone, the anvil, which in turn knocks against a curved one called the stirrup. In this way the three bones transmit the sound from the eardrum to the inner ear.

ADD A LITTLE TUBE THAT RUNS FROM THE MIDDLE EAR TO THE THROAT. THIS WILL MAKE SURE THAT THE AIR PRESSURE INSIDE THE EAR IS THE SAME AS ON THE OUTSIDE. IF THERE IS A MISMATCH, SUCH AS CAN HAPPEN WHEN YOU GO UP SOMEWHERE HIGH, THE PROBLEM WILL CORRECT ITSELF WITH A POP.

Underwater, the ear canal is full of water not air, so the eardrum does not work so well. Sound waves in the water are picked up by your jawbone and skull and get to the inner ear that way.

NOSE
The Smell Sensor

The next item on the list is as obvious as the nose on your face. In fact, it is the conk, honker, schnoz or, simply put, the nose.

The nose is nothing to sniff at. We rely on its abilities to pick up chemicals in the air – we call that smelling – to help identify rotting food and other yucky stuff that might make us ill. However, starting at the two nostrils, the nose is also the body's main air intake. Let's get nosey about your nose.

Sinuses

The nasal cavity is connected to four other air chambers called the sinuses. These are hollow air spaces inside skull bones in the forehead, cheeks, and between the eyes. The purpose of the sinuses is to cut down on the amount of bone in the skull and reduce the weight of the head. (At around 4.5 kg in adults, the head is heavy stuff!)

Flexible friend

Only the bridge of the nose – the hard ridge at the top – is made from bone (which is attached to the rest of the skull). You'll need to build the rest of the nose from layers of cartilage. Cartilage is tough stuff but much more flexible and stretchy than bone, so the nose is less likely to be damaged by knocks and bumps.

WHEN THE NOSE NEEDS A CLEAR OUT, YOU HAVE TWO OPTIONS:

1. SNIFF UP THE SNOT AND SWALLOW IT. YUM OR YUCK? THAT'S UP TO YOU, BUT THE STOMACH JUICES WILL KILL ANYTHING BAD MIXED INTO THE BLOB OF GUNK.

2. BLAST AWAY THE BLOCKAGE WITH A SNEEZE. SEE PAGE 14 FOR FULL DETAILS.

Air supply

The nose is not simply a gas pipe for air coming in and out of the body – it is a much smarter system than that. Circular muscles can expand, or 'flare', the nostrils to let more air in when needed. The air is then brushed clean of dust by a curtain of hairs before it goes to the nasal cavity.

Nasal cavity

This is the space at the top of each nostril. It is located above the roof of the mouth. Once in here, the air supply flows around a series of ridges filled with blood vessels. The heat from the blood warms the air slightly so it does not chill the windpipe and lungs.

SYSTEMS CHECK

LENGTH: *World record, Mehmet Özyürek of Italy, 8.8 cm*

FUNCTION: *Air supply and smell centre*

CONTROL: *Works on automatic but can be controlled voluntarily*

IMPORTANCE: *Very useful but not essential*

Fruity smells: Esters (alcoholic acids)

Onion-like smells: Thiols (sulphur chemicals)

Fishy smells: Amines (nitrogen-rich chemicals)

No nose is complete without snot. This slime coats the sensitive surfaces creating a barrier for germs. Your snot shield is being renewed constantly, and when you have a cold, snot production goes into overdrive to wash away any attackers. This is why your nose runs.

Smell centre

The roof of the nasal cavity has a small patch of special cells that are used for smelling. The patch is only about 3 cm long but it can pick up 10,000 unique chemicals that are mixed into the air. The nose cells are covered in chemical 'keyholes', each of which fits only one type of chemical 'key'. We can identify millions of odours from the different mixtures of chemical we breathe in.

MOUTH
The Taste Sensation

ADD PLENTY OF SALIVARY GLANDS TO THE GUMS AND UNDER THE TONGUE. THE LIQUID SALIVA SOFTENS UP THE FOOD AND MAKES IT EASIER FOR TASTE CHEMICALS TO WASH INTO THE TASTEBUDS.

A sniff of the nose is the first test we give to food. If it smells good, your mouth waters as the digestive system gets ready to do its work.

We then run a double check with our sense of taste to analyse what kind of foods are in our meal. Sweet means there is energy-giving sugar in there, and we need that to survive (and want to eat more), but a bitter taste warns there might be poisons present that will upset your tum. This crucial information is coming from sensors on the tongue and around the mouth. We'll soon lick this body part into shape.

Jaw muscles

The lower jawbone is pulled up into a bite by the masseter, a muscle on the side of the head. The masseter is the strongest muscle in the body. The crushing force of the human bite is as strong as being sat on by a horse!

SPREAD OUT THE DIFFERENT TASTEBUDS EVENLY ACROSS THE WHOLE TONGUE.

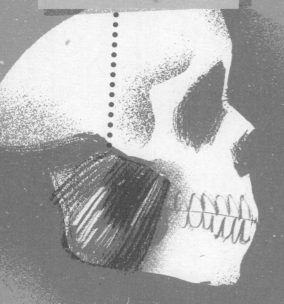

Tastebuds

Look closer at the top of the tongue. It has many tiny bumps on it, and these are where most of the taste sensors or tastebuds are located. (There are also some at the back of the throat and on the gums.) Tastebuds have tiny hollows, where food chemicals are picked up by nerve cells. The tongue can identify five tastes in food:

SALTY   BITTER   SOUR
SWEET   UMAMI
(meatiness)

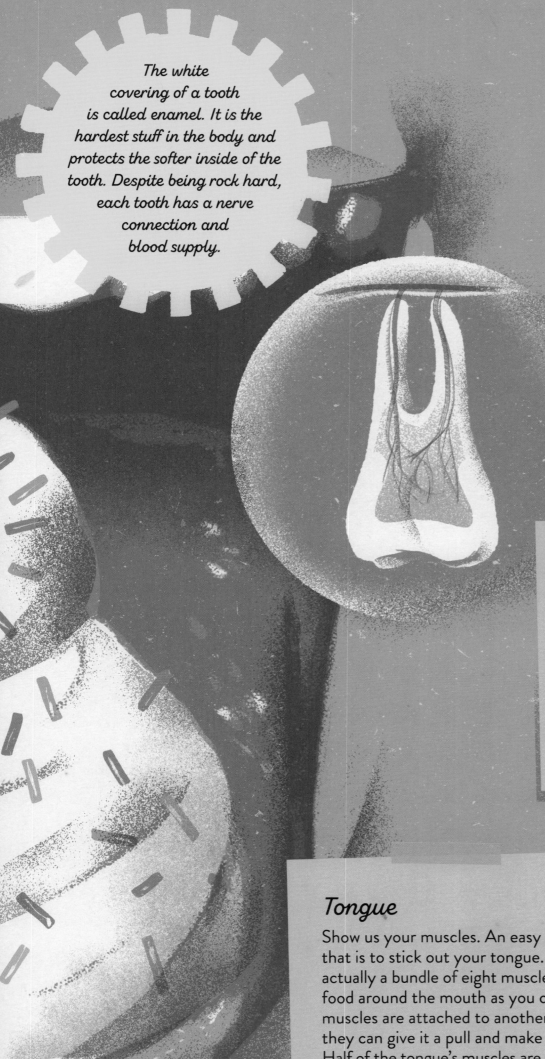

The white covering of a tooth is called enamel. It is the hardest stuff in the body and protects the softer inside of the tooth. Despite being rock hard, each tooth has a nerve connection and blood supply.

Teeth

Smile please. Let's take a look at those teeth. There are three types. The incisors at the front are sharp blades for slicing food. The pointed canine 'fangs' help grip food when you bite, and the wide, knobbly molars are there to crush up the chunks of food into a paste that is easy to swallow.

Tongue

Show us your muscles. An easy way to do that is to stick out your tongue. The tongue is actually a bundle of eight muscles, which move food around the mouth as you chew. Normally muscles are attached to another body part, so they can give it a pull and make a movement. Half of the tongue's muscles are not attached to anything and their job is to change the tongue's shape. What next? Flat, rolled or pointed?

A KID'S MOUTH IS NOT BIG ENOUGH TO FIT A FULL SET OF TEETH. START OUT BY ADDING 20 'MILK' TEETH. ONCE THE HEAD AND MOUTH ARE BIG ENOUGH, DROP THESE TEETH AND LET THE 32 ADULT TEETH GROW IN THEIR PLACE.

TOUCH
Your Feelings

We've fitted sensors for vision, hearing, smell and taste. All that is left is the fifth and final sense, the sense of touch.

Touch always comes last in a list like this. Maybe that is because it does not have an obvious body part like the eyes or ears. Instead, its sensors are spread all over the skin and throughout the insides of the body. Once you get a better look at them all, perhaps you'll get the feeling that there is a lot more to this particular sense. In fact, it is really several different sense systems working alongside each other.

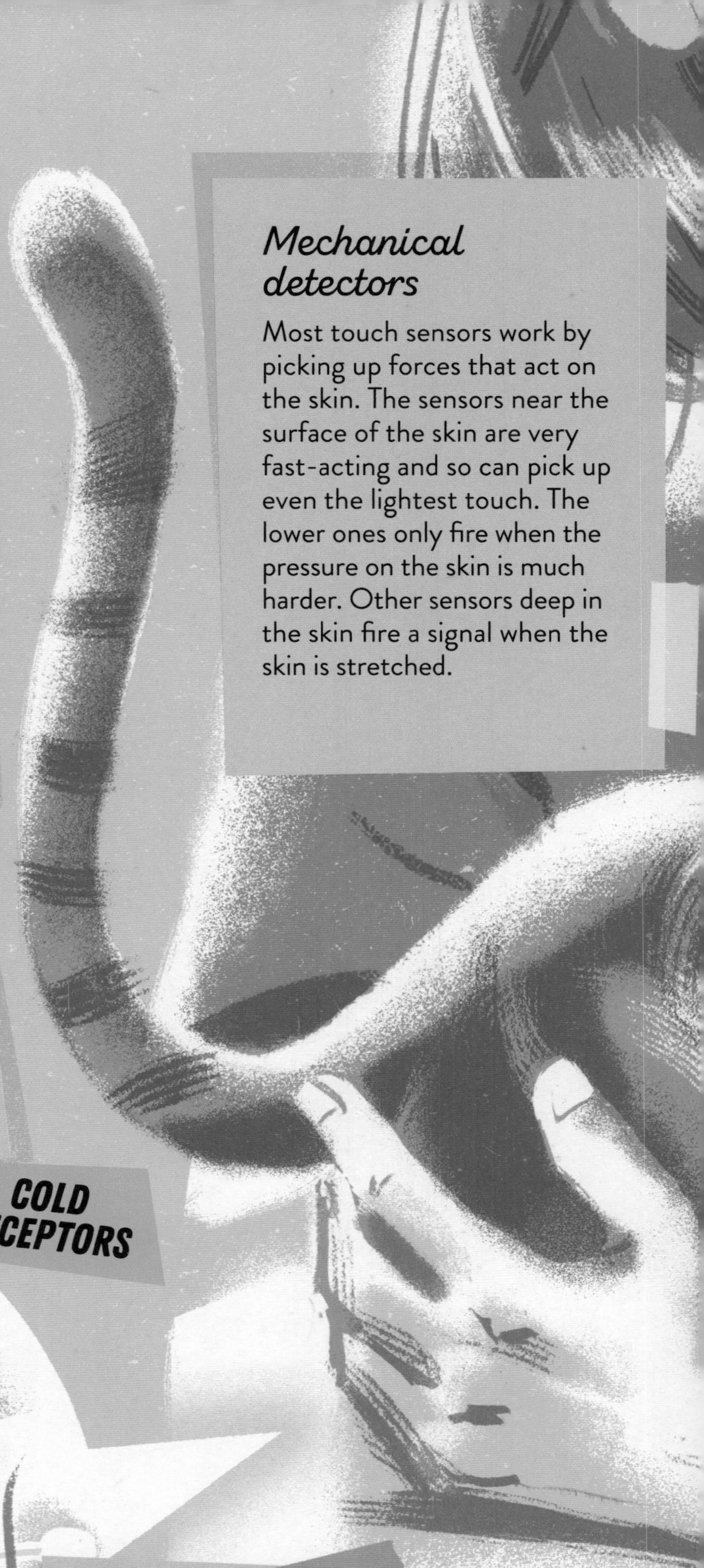

Mechanical detectors

Most touch sensors work by picking up forces that act on the skin. The sensors near the surface of the skin are very fast-acting and so can pick up even the lightest touch. The lower ones only fire when the pressure on the skin is much harder. Other sensors deep in the skin fire a signal when the skin is stretched.

Sensitivity

The touch sensors are not distributed evenly through the skin. You can check how sensitive different parts of the body are with a simple test:

Bend a paperclip into a U-shape so the ends are about 2 cm apart. Touch both ends to the palm of the hand, forearm, neck, thigh and wherever else you can reach. Do you always feel two touches? In less sensitive areas like the thigh or back you might feel only one.

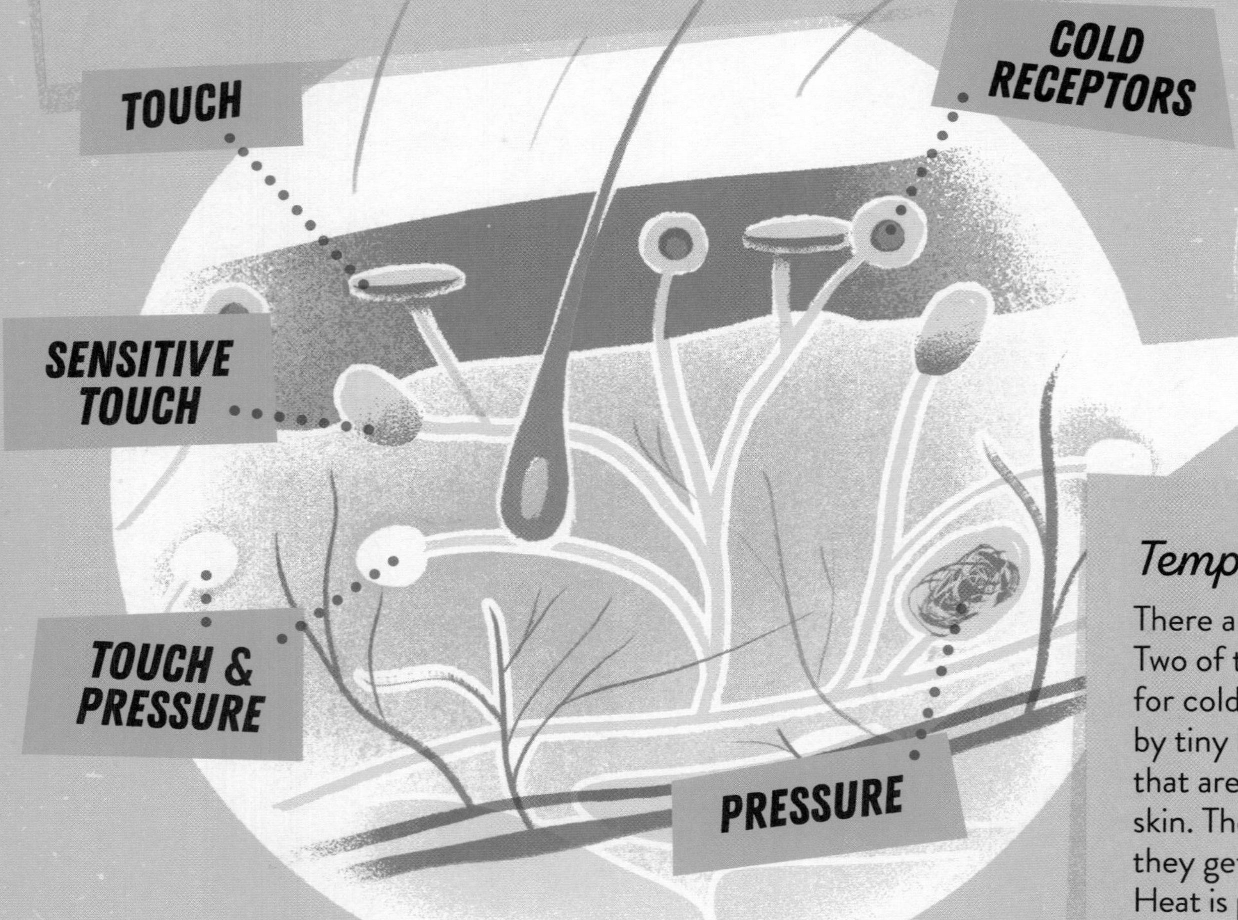

TOUCH

COLD RECEPTORS

SENSITIVE TOUCH

TOUCH & PRESSURE

PRESSURE

Temperature sensors

There are six kinds of touch sensor in the skin. Two of them are sensitive to temperature: one for cold, the other for heat. Cold is detected by tiny blob cells – called bulboid corpuscles – that are spread through the upper layer of the skin. They contain chemicals that change when they get cold, and that sends out a nerve signal. Heat is picked up by the ultrafine tips of nerves that run through the skin.

There are 3,000 touch receptors in one fingertip. The same area on the back has 30 receptors.

SYSTEMS CHECK

SIZE: *All over the body*

FUNCTION: *Senses touch and temperature; sends pain signals, and monitors body position*

CONTROL: *Automatic sense*

IMPORTANCE: *People without this sense do not realise they have injured themselves*

Body position

The sense of touch is not just about feeling what is contacting the body. Touch sensors deep in the muscles also tell the brain what position the body is in, how it is moving and how hard each body part is working.

Pain detector

The same nerve endings that pick up heat are also in charge of sending out pain signals. Anything damaging – a flame, a pinprick or a pinch on the skin, or a stinging chemical – will cause a sharp pain as a quick warning to us about the problem.

NERVOUS SYSTEM
The Communication Network

You've got a nerve! Actually you have about 220 of them, running to all corners of the body.

These nerves are the cables in a communication network which carries electrical signals that tell the brain what is going on, and then transmits back orders about what to do about it. The brain connects to the rest of the body through a thick bundle of nerves called the spinal cord. Together, these two sections make the central nervous system. A total of 72 km of nerve fibres spread out from here, connecting to every muscle, bone and organ in the body. Get the message?

Reflex

Some muscle actions happen automatically, using a system called a reflex. For example, if you touch a hot pan, your fingertip sends out a pain signal, which travels along a sensory nerve up the arm and into the spinal cord. There is no time to send a message on to the brain and wait for a response. The body already knows what to do, so the signal takes a shortcut through the spinal cord and back out along the arm's motor nerve: In less than a second, the arm muscles have pulled your finger away.

The nerves in the face and head bypass the spinal cord and connect straight to the brain.

BICEP

DENDRITE

AXON

NEURON

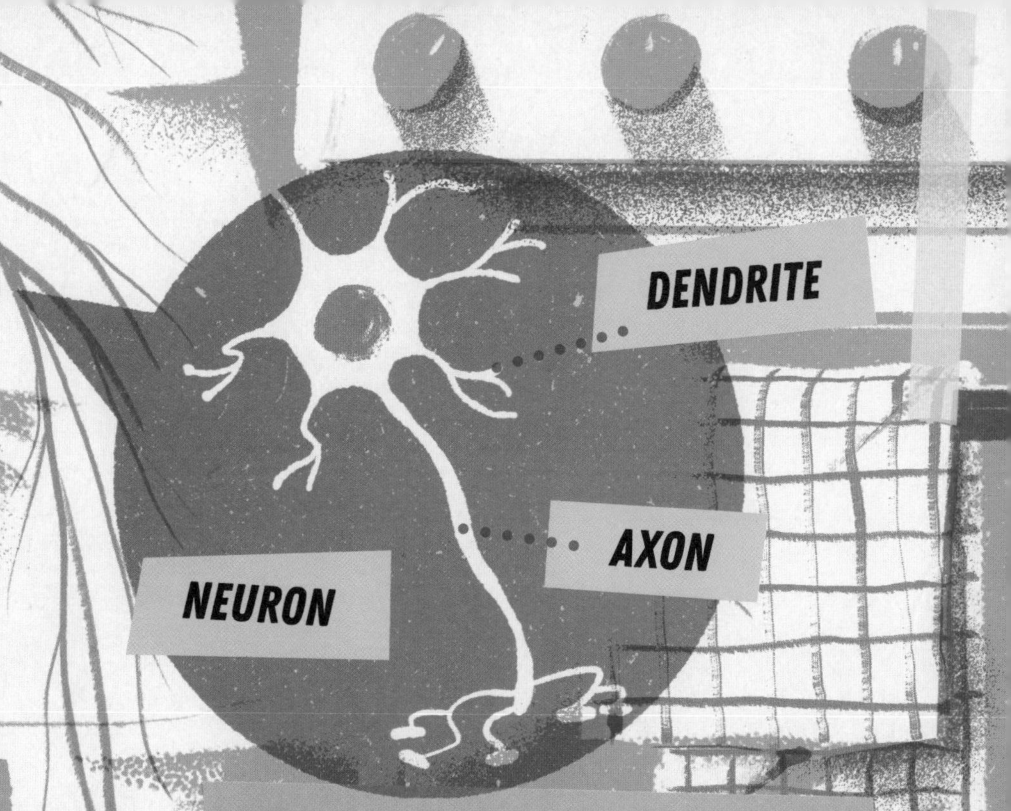

Sending signals

Nerves are wire-like fibres made up of several nerve cells, or neurons. Up close a neuron appears to be covered in branch-like extensions. These are called dendrites. They pick up signals from dozens of neighbouring neurons. The longest branch is the axon, which carries the nerve signal to the next cell along.

NERVES CARRY SIGNALS AS ELECTRICAL PULSES. COVER THE NERVES IN A LAYER OF FAT. THIS WILL ACT LIKE THE PLASTIC AROUND AN ELECTRIC WIRE, AND KEEP ALL THE ELECTRICITY ON THE INSIDE.

Inputs and outputs

Nerves are wired up to carry signals in one direction only. Sensory nerves send information from the body to the brain, including signals from the sense organs, such as eyes, ears, and nose. Motor nerves do the opposite and send commands out from the central nervous system to the muscles.

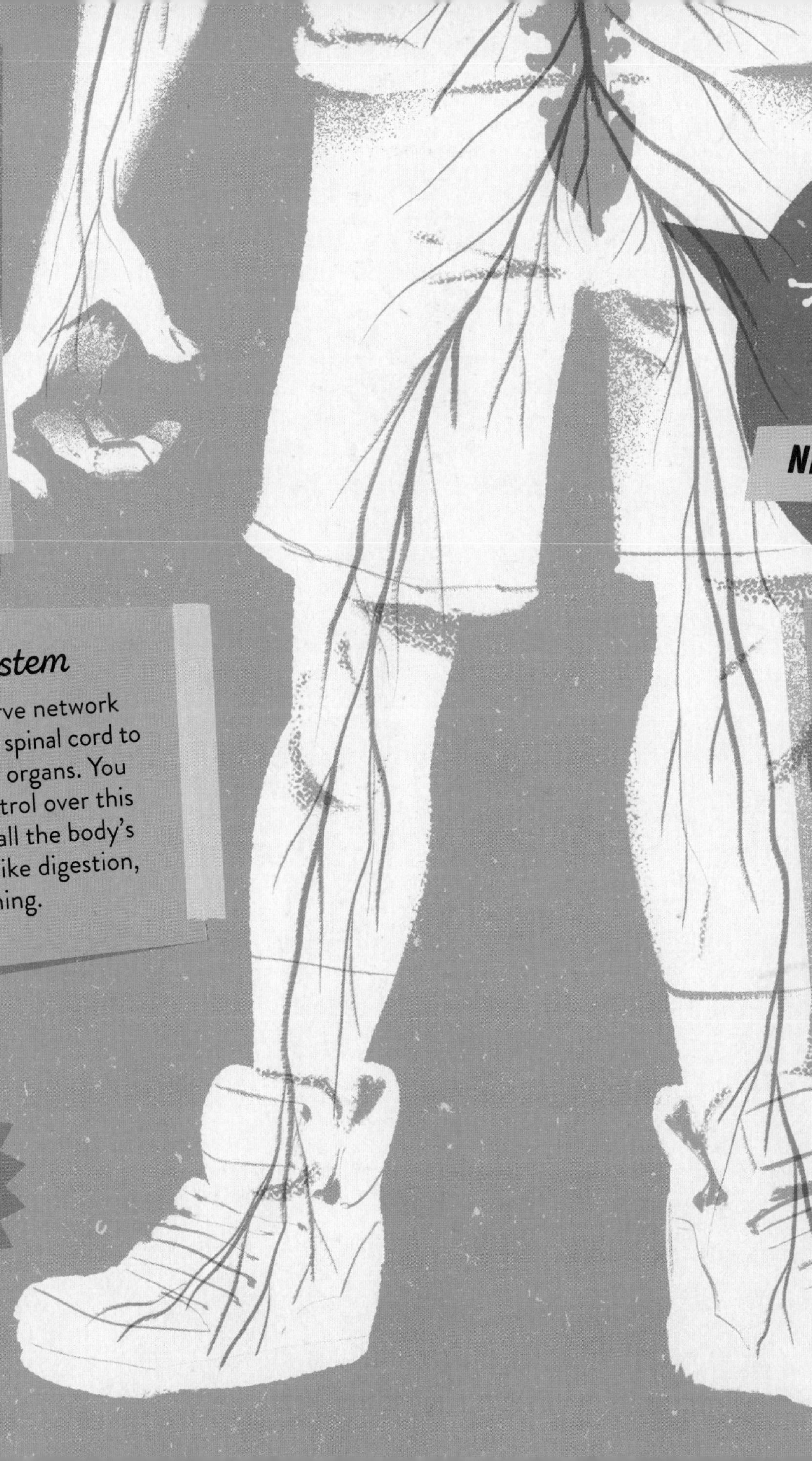

Involuntary system

There is a second nerve network that does not use the spinal cord to connect to the body organs. You do not have any control over this system, which runs all the body's automatic systems like digestion, sweating and breathing.

Nerve signals travel at about 270 km/h.

IMMUNE SYSTEM
The Defence Force

The tonsils in the back of the throat collect the germs in food and the air so the immune system can get to work in figuring out what they are as soon as possible.

Help! The body is under attack! Who are we gonna call? We need to install a team of protective bug-busters. Together they make up the immune system, which defends against outside infections.

The body is threatened by viruses, bacteria and other beasties that mean us harm, and the immune system is there to stop them getting inside the body. If germs do break in, the defence forces seek them out and destroy every last one. This part may make you feel unwell, but it is for your own good. It's them or us – your body will have to fight for its survival, so let's get prepared.

PLATELET

RED BLOOD CELL

Clotting

The skin is an essential barrier between the body and the outside world. If it gets damaged by a cut or scrape, the holes must be sealed up with a blood clot. Blood floods the area, especially tiny cells called platelets. These transform from blobs into spiky shapes so they can all cling together, thickening the blood. At the same time the platelets give out a chemical signal, which makes other materials mixed into the blood go solid and form a scab. The scab will fall off once the skin underneath has fully repaired itself.

White blood cells

As well as red blood cells, the blood also contains a large number of immune system cells, which are described as white blood cells. They are always on the look out for invading germs.

Antibodies

An invading germ will show itself because it has a different chemical marker to the body's cells. When a germ is discovered, white blood cells design a chemical flag, called an antibody, which locks onto the germ's marker. The antibodies make all the germs clump together, making them easier for other immune cells to sweep them out of the body.

GERMS

PLATELETS

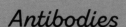

Lymph nodes

The body has a drainage system where a liquid called lymph, which gathers around muscles and organs, can trickle through tubes back into the blood supply. The immune system places filters called lymph nodes at junctions in the tube network, such as under the armpits or neck, to sift out germs and other waste. When you have an infection, the lymph nodes get busy and feel slightly swollen.

The spleen is the largest lymph node in the body, helping to destroy bacteria and other germs. It also doubles up as a factory of antibodies.

WHEN THE BODY IS UNDER ATTACK MAKE THE BODY WARMER SO THE IMMUNE CELLS CAN WORK FASTER. BE WARNED, YOUR TEMPERATURE CONTROL SYSTEM MIGHT GET CONFUSED SO YOU MAY START TO SWEAT AND SHIVER AT THE SAME TIME.

FLOOD AREAS THAT ARE UNDER ATTACK WITH WHITE BLOOD CELLS. THEY WILL SWELL UP AND BECOME TENDER BUT YOU NEED IMMUNE CELLS IN THERE FIGHTING THE GERMS.

Allergies

Sometimes the immune system overreacts, creating an allergic reaction. A common example is hayfever, which is when the body mistakes pollen grains for germs. The eyes swell up and start to water, washing out any pollen, and the nose is filled with snot to catch the pollen being breathed in.

ENDOCRINE SYSTEM
Chemical Controller

The endocrine system is a quiet player in the body, seldom seen but always at work making little changes here and there.

It works using chemical messages called hormones, which spice up the blood like the secret ingredients in soup. The nerves are reacting to events minute to minute, second to second, but over the whole day it is the hormones that are in charge: they wake you up and put you to sleep, make you hungry or feel full. The hormones are released by glands sprinkled through body. Let's install some now.

Pituitary gland

This gland has a strong link to the brain. It produces several hormones including growth hormone, which makes bones and muscles grow during childhood, and antidiuretic hormone, which controls how often you need to pee.

Adrenal gland

There are two adrenal glands, each one sitting on top of the left and right kidneys, which produce two very important hormones. Cortisol is the body's alarm system, it tells the body to prepare for an attack. Adrenalin is the emergency service, it sends a massive surge of energy so you can focus on the immediate threat.

Pineal gland

This little gland is behind the nose, hanging down from the bottom of the brain. It controls our body clock by getting information about daylight and nighttime from the eyes. As it gets dark, the gland produces a hormone called melatonin, which makes you sleepy.

Thyroid

Shaped like a butterfly, this gland can get you in a flap. It sits on the windpipe and produces a hormone called thyroxine. This is the body's speed controller. Too much and your organs work too hard and you become very restless; not enough and you become tired all the time.

USE ADRENALIN WHEN YOU HAVE TO FIGHT OFF AN ATTACKER OR RUN AWAY FROM A THREAT AS FAST AS POSSIBLE. ITS EFFECT IS CALLED THE 'FIGHT, FLIGHT OR FREEZE' RESPONSE:

- PUPILS DILATE SO YOU CAN SEE MORE CLEARLY
- THE SKIN GOES PALE AS BLOOD MOVES TO THE MUSCLES
- SINKING FEELING OCCURS IN THE STOMACH AS THE DIGESTIVE SYSTEM IS SHUTDOWN
- HEARTBEAT AND BREATHING RATE INCREASE TO KEEP THE BODY SUPPLIED WITH FUEL AND OXYGEN
- MIND GOES BLANK AS YOU CONCENTRATE ON WHAT HAPPENS NEXT
- MUSCLES TENSE UP READY FOR ACTION.

Adrenalin is not always helpful. Your muscles could be too pumped up and shaky to do delicate tasks. You can't think straight, and in extreme cases, your brain stops telling the bladder and rectum muscles to stay closed – and you make a big mess. Whoops!

SIZES OF GLAND

Pituitary - 0.5 g (pea) Pineal - 0.2 g (lentil)

Pancreas - 80 g (small banana)

Adrenal - 5 g (grape) Thyroid - 25 g (quarter of apple)

Problems with insulin production cause a disease called diabetes.

Pancreas

This is the largest gland in the body. It produces many digestive chemicals that are used by the intestines. However, it also makes insulin, which is a very important hormone that controls how much sugar is in the blood – sugar that fuels the body.

REPRODUCTIVE SYSTEM
Making Copies

It's time to add the finishing touches to the body, and introduce the copying machine, or reproductive organ.

Every human body grows from a single cell. This cell is made when two special sex cells – one from a woman and the other from a man – merge together. This is the job of the reproductive organs, and male and female versions go about it in different ways.

A sperm moves at 4 mm every minute. It needs to travel about 175 mm to find an egg – assuming it is going in the right direction!

Sex cells

Normal human cells have 46 chromosomes, which are storage racks for our genes – the instructions on how to build a body. Sex cells are unusual in that they only have 23 chromosomes. When they merge they will make a new cell with the full set of 46.

Sperm: The male sex cell is called a sperm. It is very small and has a long tail used for swimming to find a female sex cell, the egg. The sperm has nothing inside except its cargo of chromosomes.

Egg: The egg, or ovum, is hundreds of times bigger than the sperm. As well as 23 chromosomes, it has all the food reserves needed to get the new body growing. That first phase of growth will take place inside the mother's body.

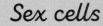

BLADDER

TESTES

Male sex organs

Sperm cells are made in two testes, which are inside the scrotum, a bag of skin that hangs between a man's legs. The sperm travel along tubes to the penis. The penis is also used for urination, but when prepared for reproduction, it fills up with extra blood, which makes it go hard and stand up straight. The penis then fits into the vagina, a tube-shaped opening to the female sex organs.

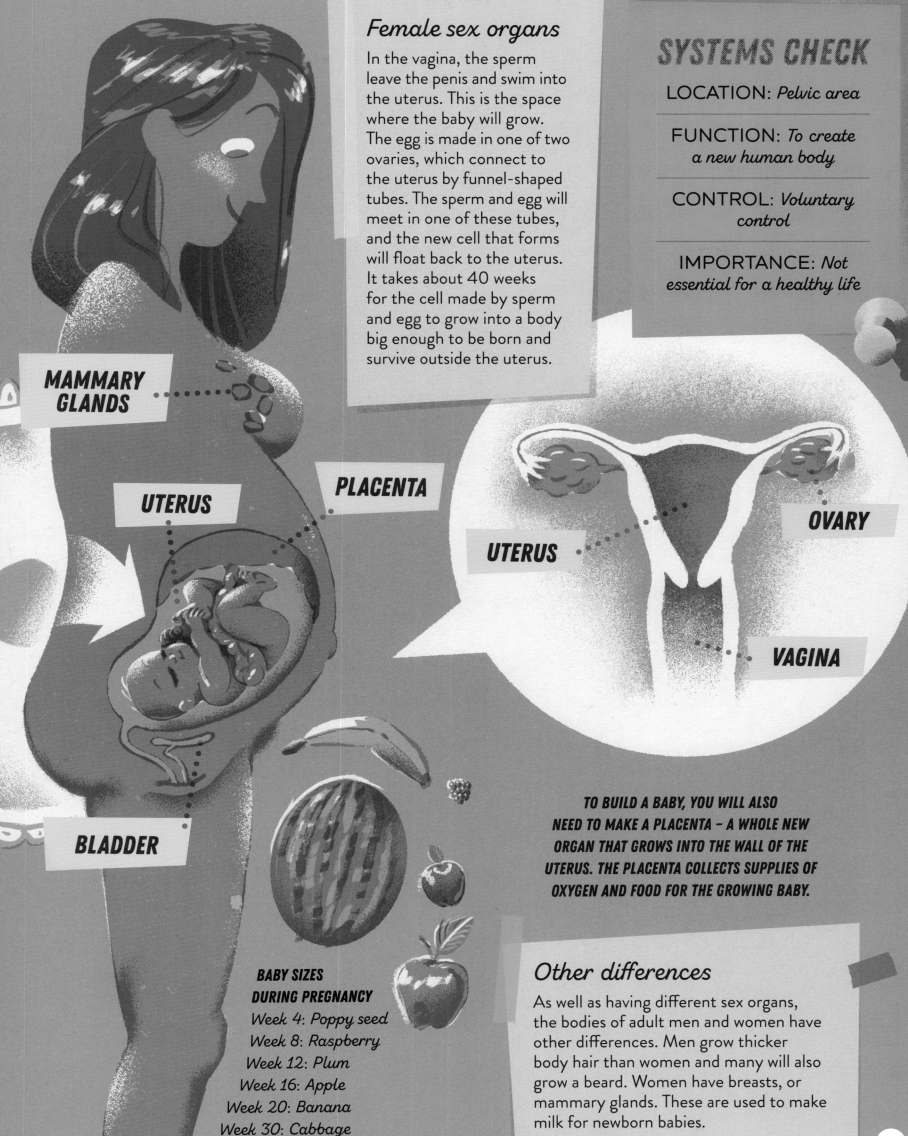

Female sex organs

In the vagina, the sperm leave the penis and swim into the uterus. This is the space where the baby will grow. The egg is made in one of two ovaries, which connect to the uterus by funnel-shaped tubes. The sperm and egg will meet in one of these tubes, and the new cell that forms will float back to the uterus. It takes about 40 weeks for the cell made by sperm and egg to grow into a body big enough to be born and survive outside the uterus.

SYSTEMS CHECK

LOCATION: *Pelvic area*

FUNCTION: *To create a new human body*

CONTROL: *Voluntary control*

IMPORTANCE: *Not essential for a healthy life*

MAMMARY GLANDS

PLACENTA

UTERUS

BLADDER

UTERUS

OVARY

VAGINA

TO BUILD A BABY, YOU WILL ALSO NEED TO MAKE A PLACENTA – A WHOLE NEW ORGAN THAT GROWS INTO THE WALL OF THE UTERUS. THE PLACENTA COLLECTS SUPPLIES OF OXYGEN AND FOOD FOR THE GROWING BABY.

BABY SIZES DURING PREGNANCY
Week 4: Poppy seed
Week 8: Raspberry
Week 12: Plum
Week 16: Apple
Week 20: Banana
Week 30: Cabbage
Week 40: Watermelon

Other differences

As well as having different sex organs, the bodies of adult men and women have other differences. Men grow thicker body hair than women and many will also grow a beard. Women have breasts, or mammary glands. These are used to make milk for newborn babies.

41

THE CELL
The Building Block

If we look closer and closer at the body, tiny units will come into focus. These are the body cells, which are like the bricks that build every body part.

The human body uses hundreds of different kinds of cell: the blood cell, skin cell, nerve cell and muscle cell are all built to perform a particular job. However, inside each type of cell, they all rely on the same set of tiny machines – called organelles – to keep them working. Take a good look now.

A typical human cell is about a hundredth of a millimetre wide. It would take about 2,500 to cover this full stop
→ .

Endoplasmic reticulum

Proteins and other important chemicals are built inside the endoplasmic reticulum, which is a network of tubes surrounding the nucleus. The instructions for building proteins are sent here from the nucleus.

Membrane

This is an ultrafine layer of fat – only about 10 billionths of a metre thick – that surrounds every cell. The membrane acts like a bag, holding the cell's liquid. The liquid is called cytoplasm and it is mostly water with hundreds of chemicals mixed into it.

Golgi apparatus

This is a stack of membranes that bags up chemicals, such as hormones, to be released from the cell. Little spheres of membrane with the chemicals locked inside are called vesicles. They form by breaking off from the edges of this organelle.

Lysosome

Even a cell produces waste. It is cleared away using a lysosome, which is a bag of cleaning chemicals. Anything that goes inside the lysosome gets cut up into simple substances that can be recycled by the cell.

You are not alone. There are 39 trillion bacteria living on and in your body. That is 9 trillion more than your actual body cells, although bacteria are hundreds of times smaller than human cells. Most of them live in the intestines and help with digestion.

SYSTEMS CHECK

LENGTH: *from 30 to 100 micrometres*

FUNCTION: *Smallest unit of the body*

CONTROL: *Survive by working as part of an organised team*

IMPORTANCE: *Cells are dying all the time, but humans need about 30 trillion of them to live*

Mitochondria

These little nuggets are the cell's power stations. They take the sugars and fats supplied by the digestive system and burn them using oxygen from the lungs. The energy released allows the cell to build other complex chemicals, such as proteins.

Nucleus

The largest organelle, this holds the cell's DNA – short for deoxyribonucleic acid. DNA carries genes, or coded instructions on how to build the cell, or any other cell needed in the human body.

YOU WILL NEED TO INCLUDE MORE MITOCHONDRIA IN CELLS THAT USE A LOT OF ENERGY. MUSCLE CELLS WILL HAVE HUNDREDS OF THEM.

Vesicle

The vesicle travels to the main membrane around the cell to release the hormone. There it merges with the membrane, and the chemical inside is pushed out.

DNA
Coded Instructions

Well done! You've built yourself a human body. But what happens if someone does not have this book to guide them?

Luckily a human body is clever enough to build itself. It has all the information it needs in every cell nucleus. Inside are long strands of a chemical called deoxyribonucleic acid (but luckily we can shorten this name to DNA). The instructions for building a body, also called your genes, are stored as a code on the DNA, and your body has a unique set. None of the other 7.7 billion people on Earth has the same genetic code as you! Let's unravel what is going on.

Gene

A gene is a section of DNA that contains the code to build one protein. That section of DNA is copied onto a movable form called RNA (ribonucleic acid), and that goes to the endoplasmic reticulum (see p42–43). There its code is used to build a protein needed by the cell.

Genome

The complete set of genes in a cell is called the human genome. There are about 20,000 genes needed to build a human body. Although everyone's body is different in things like height, weight, and colour of hair, skin and eyes, most of our genes are more or less the same. All of our differences come from just 100 of our genes.

DNA IS VERY FLIMSY STUFF, WHICH IS WHY IT IS STORED OUT OF THE WAY IN THE NUCLEUS. BE SURE TO COIL IT CAREFULLY AROUND THE CHROMOSOME STORAGE SYSTEMS PROVIDED.

Double helix

As its name suggests, DNA is a complicated chemical. It forms a long spiral ladder shape called a double helix. The sides of the ladder are made from a sugar called ribose. The 'rung' sections are made from the nucleic acid parts of DNA.

Every cell nucleus has about 2 metres of DNA packed inside. If you took all of the DNA in a human body and strung it together, it would stretch across the whole solar system twice over!

Code letters

There are four types of nucleic acid in DNA: thyamine, guanine, adenine and cytosine, which are simplified to T, G, A, and C. These four always pair up to make the rung sections of the DNA helix; T always connects with A and G with C. Rung after rung, these chemicals spell out the genetic code using these four letters.

Enzymes

Nearly all the proteins made by the cell are used as enzymes. Enzymes are tiny chemical machines that organise all the processes in a cell. Each enzyme has a particular shape which allows it to fit exactly around its target chemicals, like a key in a lock. Enzymes are used to digest food and build new cells.

G

T

C

C

A

G

45

GLOSSARY

Antibody

A special protein produced by the white blood cells, which signal the immune system to start fighting infections in the body.

Cell

The basic building block of plants and animals (and humans of course!). There are 100 trillion cells in a human, and each one contains all the information necessary to make a human being.

Central nervous system

The collection of nerves in the brain and spinal cord that control the activity of the whole body.

Chromosome

The structure in a cell that contains the genetic information. It is made of DNA and protein.

Circulatory system

The system that moves blood, oxygen and nutrients through the body. It is made up of the heart, arteries, capillaries and veins.

Digestive system

The system of organs that get food into and out of the body, and use the food to keep the body healthy. It includes the mouth, salivary glands, oesophagus, stomach, liver, gallbladder, pancreas, small intestine, colon and rectum.

DNA

This stands for deoxyribonucleic acid. It is a molecule that makes up the chromosomes found in almost all cells. It contains the genetic code that determines the characteristics of a living thing, and tells it how to develop and function.

Endocrine system

The system of glands that make the body's hormones. The major glands that make up this system are the hypothalamus, pituitary, thyroid, adrenals, pineal, ovaries, testes and pancreas (which is also part of the digestive system).

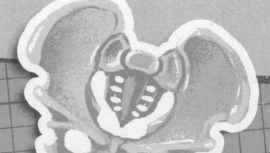

Enzyme

A special type of protein, responsible for a lot of stuff going on in cells. Enzymes help speed up chemical reactions.

Excretory system

The system of the body that processes and gets rid of waste products such as sweat and urine. The parts of the body involved are the sweat glands, the liver, the lungs and the kidney system.

Gene

Genes carry the information that determines what you look like and who you are. They are found in chromosomes.

Hormone

Chemical substances produced in the body and secreted by glands that control various functions in the body like growth and reproduction.

Immune system

The body's natural defence system which fights germs and infections.

Lymphatic system

The tissues and organs (such as bone marrow, spleen, thymus and lymph nodes) in the body that produce and store cells that fight infection and disease. It is part of the immune system.

Neuron

Each nerve is made up of many cells called neurons. Neurons communicate with each other through electrical signals.

Organelle

Organelles form part of the cell, and work like tiny machines to keep each cell working. Organelle means 'little organ'.

Protein

There are thousands of different proteins in the human body, every cell uses proteins to perform many types of jobs.

Reproductive system

The system in males and females that allows reproduction of the species.

Respiratory system

The system of organs that are involved in breathing. These include the nose, throat, larynx, trachea, bronchi and lungs.

INDEX

MUSCLES

BONES

P

PO

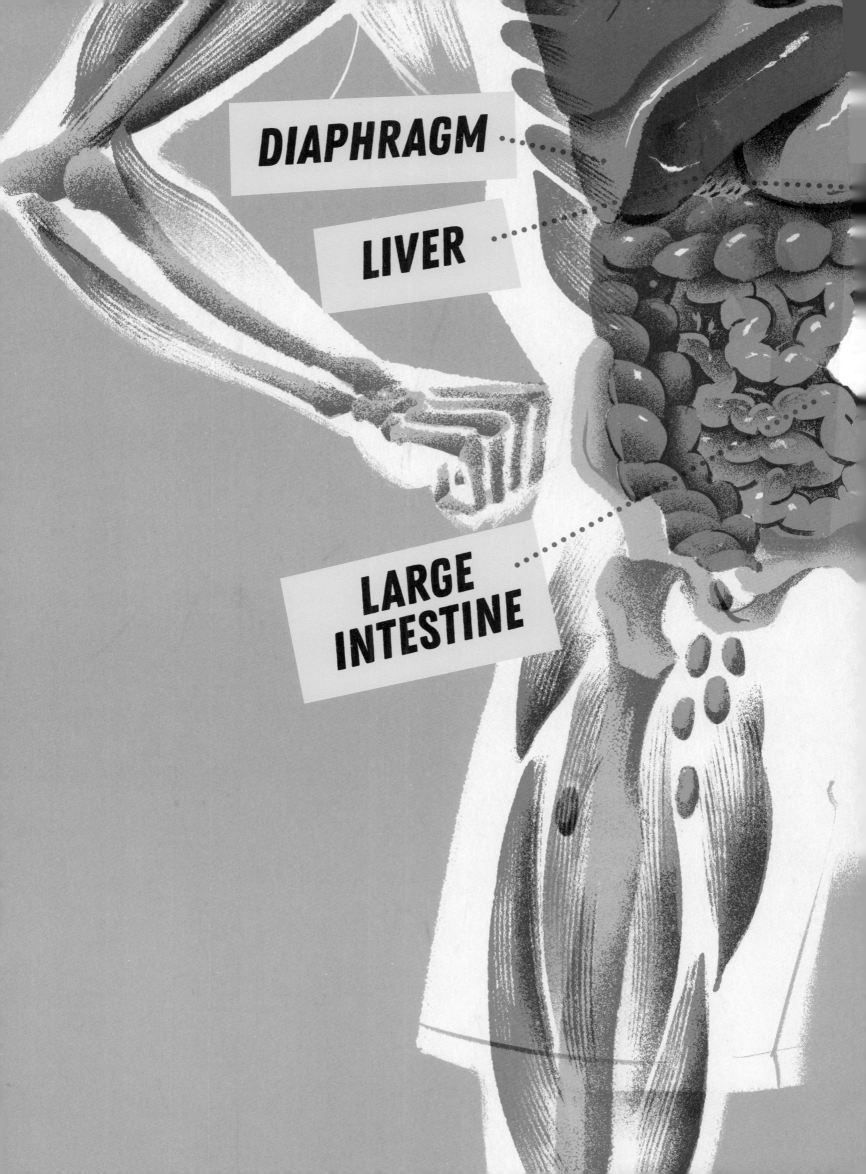

DIAPHRAGM

LIVER

LARGE
INTESTINE

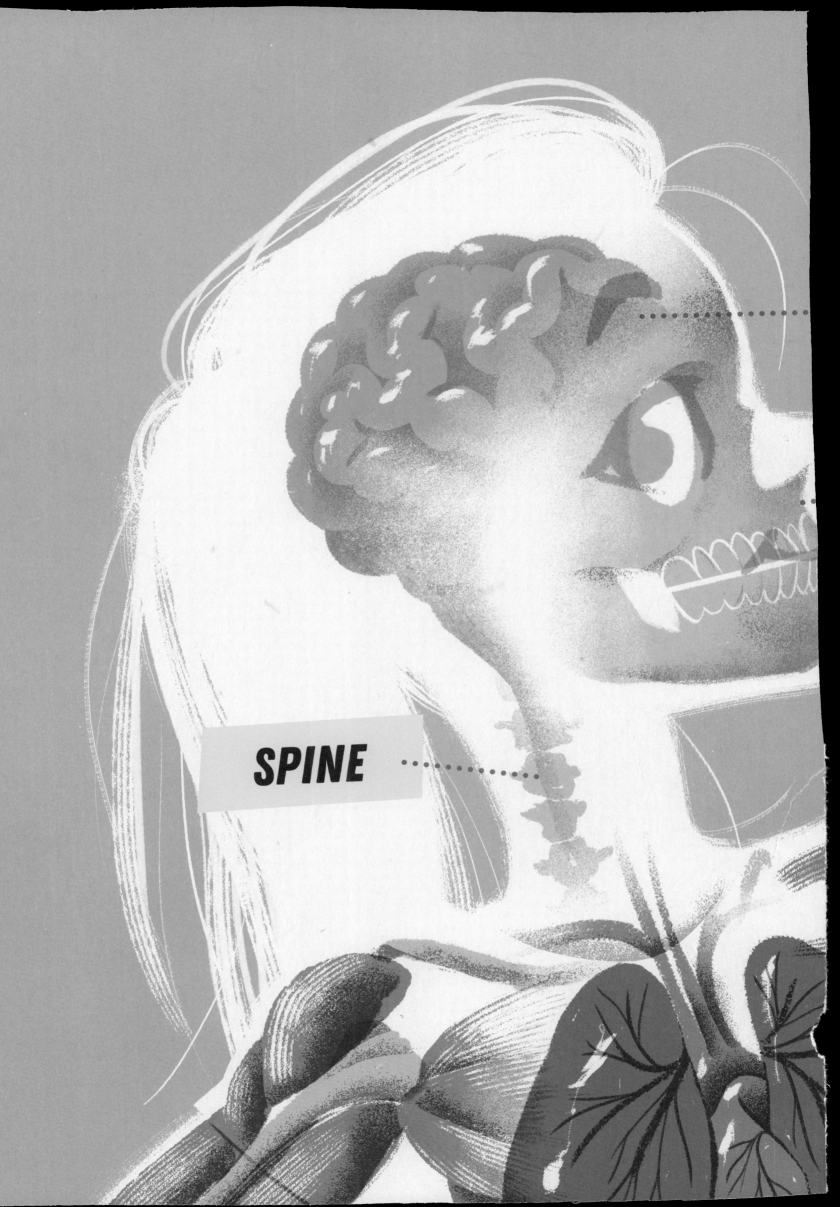

SPINE

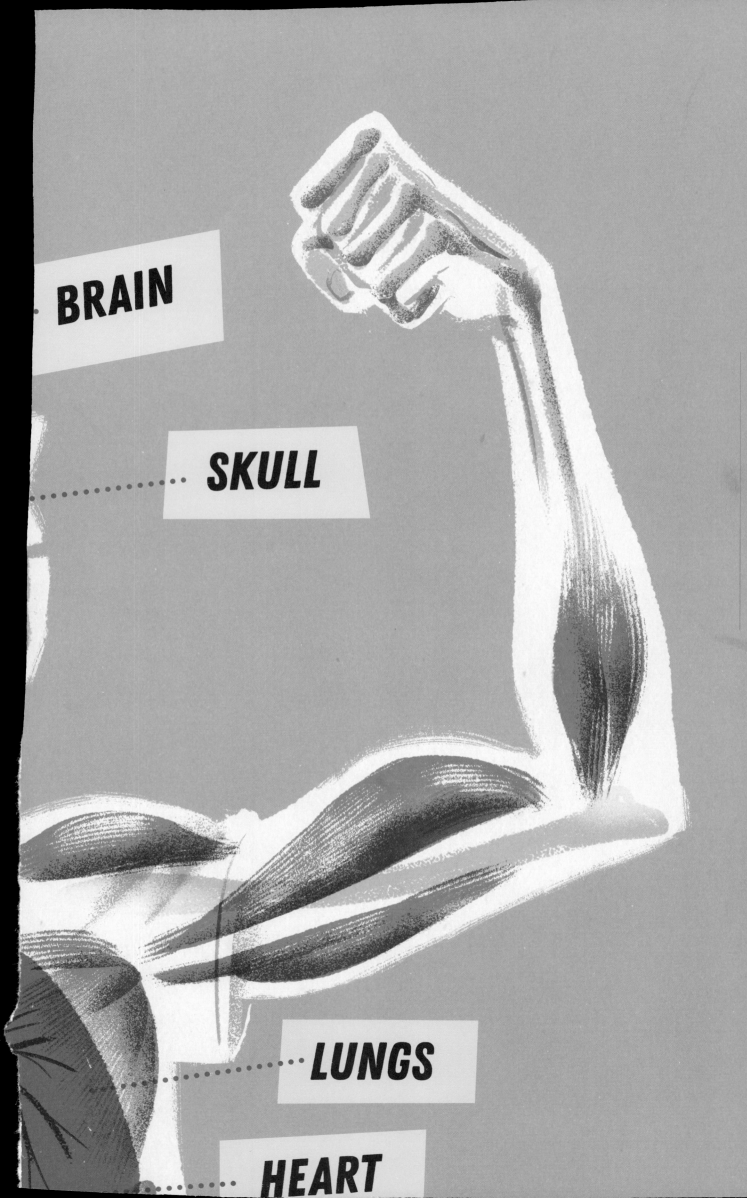

BRAIN

SKULL

LUNGS

HEART

ITEMS INCLUDED

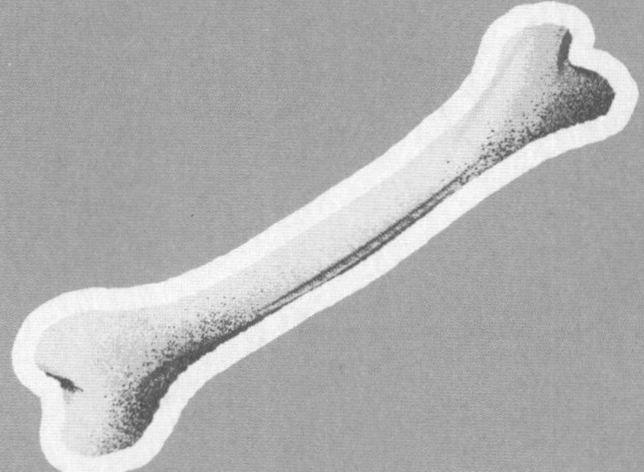

x 206

x 650 (APPROX.)

x 51*

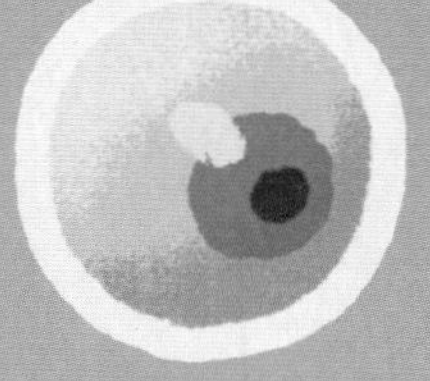

x 2

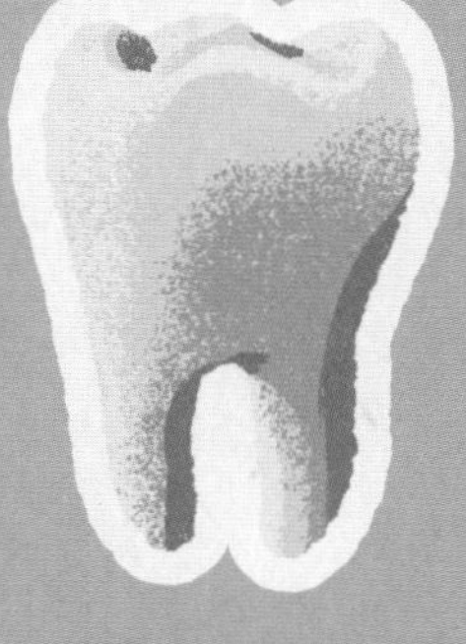

x 32*

*IN ADULTS

LYMPH NODES

SMALL INTESTINE

PANCREAS

STOMACH

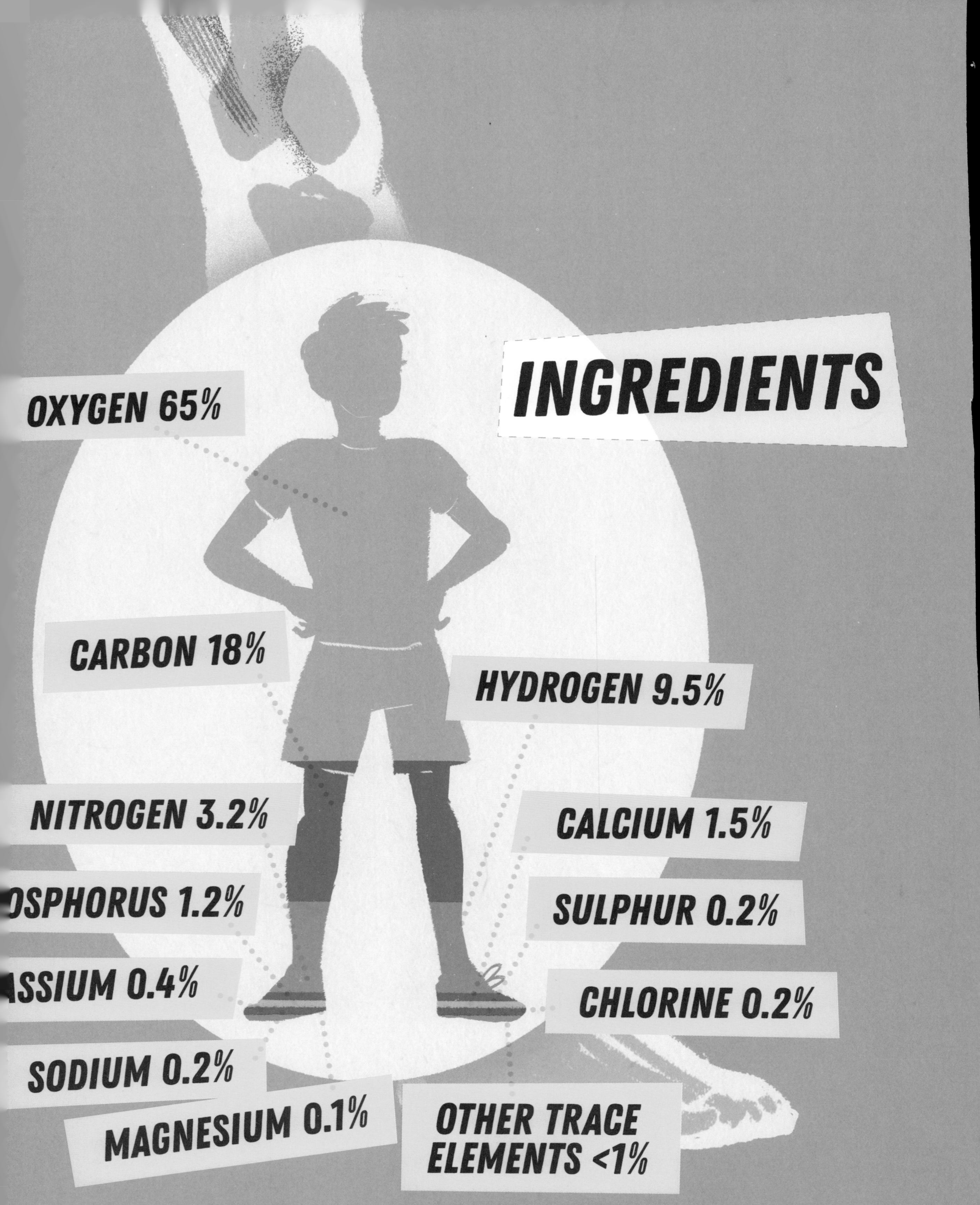

INGREDIENTS

OXYGEN 65%

CARBON 18%

HYDROGEN 9.5%

NITROGEN 3.2%

CALCIUM 1.5%

OSPHORUS 1.2%

SULPHUR 0.2%

ASSIUM 0.4%

CHLORINE 0.2%

SODIUM 0.2%

MAGNESIUM 0.1%

OTHER TRACE
ELEMENTS <1%